DITCHING ABANDONMENT

Live in the Freedom, Fullness and Fulfillment You Deserve

DITCHING ABANDONMENT

Live in the Freedom, Fullness and Fulfillment You Deserve

by:

DR. TANESHA LAWRENCE, MD

Copyright © 2024 by Dr. Tanesha Lawrence, MD

All rights reserved. Except permitted under the U.S. Copyright Act of 1976, no part of this publication may be used, reproduced, distributed or transmitted by in any form or by any means, graphic, electronic or mechanical or stored in a database or retrieval system, without the prior written permission to the publisher except in the case of brief quotations embodied in critical articles and reviews.

Unless otherwise indicated, Scriptures are taken from the Holy Bible, New International Version®, NIV® Copyright © 1973, 1978, 1984, 2011 by Biblica, Inc.™ Used by permission. All rights reserved worldwide.

Scripture taken from the Amplified Bible (AMP), Copyright © 1954, 1958, 1962, 1964, 1965, 1987 by The Lockman Foundation. Used by permission.

Scripture quotations are from the ESV® Bible (The Holy Bible, English Standard Version®), © 2001 by Crossway, a publishing ministry of Good News Publishers. Used by permission. All rights reserved. The ESV text may not be quoted in any publication made available to the public by a Creative Commons license. The ESV may not be translated in whole or in part into any other language.

Scripture quotations marked (NRSV) are taken from the New Revised Standard Version Bible, copyright © 1989 National Council of the Churches of Christ in the United States of America. Used by permission. All rights reserved worldwide.

Vine Publishing's name and logo are trademarks of Vine Publishing, Inc.

ISBN: 979-8-9891446-2-4 (paperback)
ISBN: 979-8-9891446-3-1 (e-book)

Library of Congress Cataloging-in-Publication Data
Library of Congress Control Number: 2024916484

Published by Vine Publishing, Inc.
New York, NY
www.vinepublish.com

Printed in the United States of America

MEDICAL DISCLAIMER:

Dr. Tanesha Lawrence, MD is a board-certified family medicine physician who practices in both family medicine, urgent care medicine and emergency medicine. Although she does engage with different aspects of mental health disease and mental health treatment modalities in varying practice environments, she is not nor does she claim to be a licensed psychiatrist, psychologist or mental health professional. The information given by Dr. Tanesha Lawrence, MD, and any other affiliates is not intended or implied to be a substitute for professional medical or mental health advice, diagnosis or treatment. All content, including text, graphics, images and information, contained on or available through this book is for general information purposes only—some based on Dr. Lawrence's personal opinions and experiences and some based on research.

Dr. Tanesha Lawrence, MD and any other affiliates make no representation and assumes no responsibility for the accuracy of information contained in or available through this book and such information is subject to change without notice. You are encouraged to confirm any information obtained from or through this book with other sources, and review all information regarding any mental health conditions, medical conditions or treatment with your physician. Never disregard professional medical advice or delay seeking medical treatment including but not limited to mental health treatment because of something you have read on or accessed through this book.

Dr. Tanesha Lawrence, MD and any affiliates does not recommend, endorse or make any representation about the efficacy, appropriateness or suitability of any specific tests, products, procedures, treatments, services, opinions, health care providers or other information that may be contained in this book.

Dr. Tanesha Lawrence, MD, and any affiliates are not responsible nor liable for any advice, course of treatment, diagnosis or any other information, services or products that you obtain.

DEDICATION

I dedicate this book to some of the most important people in my life—the ones who I fondly call, *"The Committee."* Thank you for loving me the way you do. My life is better because of you.

TABLE OF CONTENTS

Acknowledgment .... *xi*

Introduction *1*

SECTION 1: IN THE BEGINNING . . .

Chapter 1: God's Intentions . . . The Genesis 7

Chapter 2: My Story..17

SECTION 2: ROOT CAUSES OF ABANDONMENT ISSUES

Chapter 3: Root Causes of Abandonment..................................25

Chapter 4: Abandonment and Identity 39

SECTION 3: EFFECTS OF ABANDONMENT ISSUES

Chapter 5: Shame...55

Chapter 6: Fear and Anxiety 61

Chapter 7: Imposter Syndrome 71

Chapter 8: Special Circumstances of Abandonment 77

Chapter 9: Steps to Victory 83

Chapter 10: Conclusion...93

Bibliography *97*

Notes... *101*

Additional Informative Resources:.. *109*

ACKNOWLEDGMENT

I give all glory, praise and honor to God the Father, Jesus Christ the Son and the Holy Spirit for who they are and their love for me. I am truly grateful for the grace, love, faithfulness and provision of God. Without Him, I would not be who I am today, nor would I have been able to write this book. God, thank you for your healing, deliverance and breakthrough in so many areas of my life, and the revelation of the lessons that I can now share with others. If I had 10,000 tongues, it would not be enough to praise your holy name. May you continually be glorified through me.

I'm thankful for the Committee—those five precious parental figures that God has used to raise me, shape me, guide me, and love me beyond what I deserve. To my mom (June), dad (Andrew), mommy (Cherry), daddy (Derrick), and May May (grandma—God rest her soul)—thank you, thank you, thank you for all you have done and continue to do for me. I could never repay you, but I hope to continue to show you that your love and investment have not been in vain. I am grateful that God has blessed me with you.

Special thanks to my amazing siblings, Annie, Adrian, Drew and Dana, who continue to hold me down. Thanks for being a safe space, for your wisdom, laughs, support and so much more through the years. I love you all.

To my beloved Kevin, my special needs brother, who can't read or understand this, but whose presence in my life is significant nonetheless and who is still worth mentioning: Kev, I'm so glad that God has brought you a mighty long way. Thank you for helping to shape my character, showing me how to love and serve others, and making me a better person overall through participating in your care. I love you, and may the Lord continue to keep you and bring you greater deliverance and peace in the years to come.

I want to thank my spiritual mentors, guides, and role models—whether intentionally or unintentionally—who have been significant in my spiritual journey: My pastor, the Rev. Dr. Elaine McCullins Flake; Pastor Emeritus Floyd H. Flake; Dr. Kevin D. Miller; Dr. Rob Reimer; Dr. Martin Sanders (God rest his soul); Dr. Stanley John; Dr. Ron Walborn; Dr. Mike Plunkett; and Rev. Terrence McKinley—specifically for your example, leadership, impact, and shaping of my life, especially in spiritual transformation in different ways. I would also like to thank Rev. Julia Russell, Rev. Nicole Edness, Rev. Greta Gainer Anderson, First Lady Myra Miller, and Sis. Blossom Ferguson, especially for your prayers and

ACKNOWLEDGEMENT

your example of living Christ. Thank you to my good family friend Junie McLeod and my cousin Sharon Smith, who God used in a crucial way at a pivotal time in my life to steer me off the road to destruction. To all of you, whether for a season or on an ongoing basis, whether openly or through your private prayers, know that God has used you in important ways in my journey to shape, mold, challenge, teach, inspire, and impact me. I am truly grateful.

Thank you to my sister-friend, Vine Publishing founder and CEO, Rev. Taneki Dacres, for your guidance in bringing this book to life and for doing so with wisdom and excellence. I'm so thankful for your friendship and for your gifts that are a blessing to me in so many ways.

Thank you to my extended family—aunts, uncles, cousins, and so forth around the world—who are the best family I could ever have. Blood and non-blood relatives, thank you for embracing me and loving me the way you do, from the time I was a little girl running in the yard until now. I appreciate your support, prayers, and love always.

I am thankful to the ancestors who have gone before me, laid the foundation, and made sacrifices so that I could live a better life. I especially want to thank three significant people who have gone on to be with the Lord, but who I know are instrumental in the blessings I enjoy now. I thank God for my maternal grandmother, May May, who literally worked, sacrificed, and gave everything she had to ensure I had the best. May May, I love and miss you so much. I look forward to seeing you again one day, and I am forever grateful for your sacrifice for me and the rest of the family. I also thank God for my paternal grandmother, Hilda, and my maternal great-grandmother, Ms. Lattie, who were praying, God-fearing women. They prayed for me and many others in the family, and I know their prayers have shaped the trajectory of my life to my benefit.

Segun, you have taught me a lot and God has used you to help shape and develop me into who I am today. Thank you for your presence in my life.

To my village of friends, sister-friends, and brother-friends— too many to name—that God has blessed me with through the years: My life is simply more full because of you. In a world where people complain of a lack of authentic and valid friendships, I am so blessed to say that is not my experience.

INTRODUCTION

Most if not every one of us have experienced being abandoned in one form or another—either by family, friends, spouses, boyfriends, girlfriends, and/or colleagues. Throughout history and even today, leaders and governments who have persecuted their citizens or mistreated certain groups in society have, in essence, abandoned those individuals. When you think about it, abandonment (the state of being abandoned) is a part of life, and a little abandonment here and there usually does not significantly impact most people in a negative way. However, there are some of us who have felt abandoned, and others who have truly suffered not only repeated abandonment but such devastating abandonment that it has significantly altered who we are, left us with dysfunctional behavioral traits, and kept us from the freedom and joy God wants us to have. Abandonment, if not dealt with, can have a debilitating impact on one's life.

I've always thought that the word abandon simply meant "to leave." I've always thought that it meant "the feeling of being left behind" or something along those lines. However, upon further research, I've discovered the depth of the word. In particular, Merriam-Webster Dictionary's definition blew my mind. The dictionary defines it as, "To withdraw protection, support, or help from" or "To give up with the intent of never again claiming a right or interest in."[1] Whew! Think about that definition for a minute. "To withdraw protection or support; to never claim rights or interest in." Wow . . . I don't know about you, but just the thought of being unprotected, unsupported, and unwanted elicits internal emotional turmoil in me. No one wants to experience being abandoned, and yet many feel abandoned. However, I've discovered that there is a difference between feeling abandoned and true abandonment.

> *Community and healthy relationships bring joy and breathe life. To be abandoned is to be left breathless, gasping for the breath of belonging and acceptance.*

Perceived abandonment, one that is grounded in the feeling of being neglected, has the power to limit us severely. Individuals who have experienced real abandonment, as well those who have perceived abandonment, run the risk of suffering from abandonment issues—which refers to "emotional difficulties that someone might experience because of their anxiety or fear of being abandoned."[2] Although it is not an official mental health or psychiatric diagnosis,

INTRODUCTION

abandonment issues typically involve a "strong fear of losing loved ones or of them leaving a relationship"[3] and is often associated with the term fear of abandonment. "This fear can result from trauma, anxiety disorders, and other mental health conditions."[4] The sad truth is that many people have abandonment issues and are not aware of it. This is why I wrote this book.

Ditching Abandonment was written to bring awareness to the issue of abandonment—an issue that has afflicted countless people. Abandonment has been a silent plague—robbing us of our joy, our peace, and our healthy relationships. Abandonment has killed dreams, stifled purpose, and crushed freedom. Without even knowing it, I lived under the bondage of abandonment issues for years, unaware of what it was and its effect on my life. That is, until God, in His mercy, connected me to a former seminary professor who has become a dear friend, Dr. Rob Reimer, and to Soul Care, his inner healing ministry.[5]

It was through Dr. Reimer's Soul Care ministry that I began to understand abandonment and how it related to my unhealthy mindset, poor emotional state, and spiritual fatigue. The principles taught liberated me from the bondage of abandonment, and that's my hope for you.

Ditching Abandonment uncovers the depths and effects of abandonment. In it, I present God's intentions for humanity to be made whole; unveil my own story; highlight situations that open the doors to abandonment issues; expose the resulting identity crisis, shame, fear, and anxiety; and so much more. Together, we will journey through the hills and valleys of abandonment. And at the end of this literary journey, you will be led to the steps to victory. Are you ready?

As you read this book, I encourage you to read it with an open mind, heart, and spirit. Pray and ask God for revelation. Ask God to uncover, reveal, and uproot. Perhaps there are some experiences that you have buried deep within your soul; ask God to bring them to the surface. Be prepared for the Spirit of God—the Holy Spirit—to "speak" and show you things you may have never seen or considered. As God speaks, write. Grab a notebook or an electronic device and write down all that you are hearing and discovering as you read. Finally, don't rush. You may need to reread certain sections or read in small chunks to fully digest all the information provided. Don't be surprised by new revelation and self-discovery with multiple readings of this book.

Wrestle with your thoughts; grapple with the sections that are most challenging for you. Pray and ask God questions. If needed, discuss what you are struggling with or feeling with a trusted friend or advisor. It is my sincere hope and prayer that at the conclusion of this book, no matter what you have faced, no matter who has said you are unworthy, or if you have falsely believed you are abandoned and have lived as such, you will know that God designed you to live in freedom and wholeness. May you no longer live under the shadow of abandonment, and instead live in the fullness of your God-ordained identity.

SECTION 1

IN THE BEGINNING . . .

CHAPTER 1:

GOD'S INTENTIONS . . .THE GENESIS

*The LORD is near to the brokenhearted
and saves the crushed in spirit. (Psalm 34:18 ESV)*

I'll begin this chapter by making a concrete statement, one that I believe is a foundational truth. Here it is: It was never God's intention for us to experience abandonment. Never. God in His mysterious nature is a relational being. It is my faith belief that God is a Triune God—that is, God exists in three Divine Beings. This is also known as the Holy Trinity—God the Father, Jesus the Son, and the Holy Spirit—all in perfect union with each other. It is this Triune God who together formed the mountains and valleys, the lakes, rivers, and seas. It is this all-powerful God who created human beings into His own image and imparted the breath of life into all humanity. God the Father, Jesus the Son, and the Holy Spirit are in perfect relationship working in and through creation. Among the Godhead, there is no malice, competition, hurt, backbiting, envy, jealousy, judgment, or hypocrisy—just pure love. Our God is truly relational, and it was and still is the Creator's intention to never have us experience abandonment. How do we know this? Well, let's start with Adam and Eve, God's first couple on the earth, as referenced in the Bible.

The first biblical book, Genesis, presents to us the creation story. It is there that we discover the Holy Trinity choosing to create the universe, the earth, and humanity. Now, I used the word *choose* because God is the superiorly perfect being, completely fulfilled in Himself. As such, He did not need us, or need our love, to be fulfilled. Yet God chose to create humanity "because it pleased Him to bring into being creatures that would share in the love He has always had for His Son through the love-bond of the Spirit."[6] In other words, God created us to experience His love and to experience the beauty of the perfect love that flows between God the Father, Jesus the Christ, and the Holy Spirit. He cherishes us so much that He wants to have an intimate relationship with us where we will grow to love Him in a truly deep and authentic way. Super relational.

When God decided to create Eve for the man, Adam, the Bible tells us that "the Lord God said, 'It is not good that the man should be alone; I will make him a helper as his partner'" (Gen. 2:18, NRSV). In that moment, God created human connection and human love. God in His omniscience knew the importance of human relationships, and so He created Adam and Eve to live in harmony—in union with each other but also in unrestricted relationship with their Creator. Together, Adam and Eve walked and talked with God. They never felt abandoned by God or abandoned by each other. They had the privilege of experiencing

GOD'S INTENTIONS . . .THE GENESIS

the full presence of God. Unlike our current human reality, they could see, feel, touch, hear, and experience God with all of their senses and with every part of their being. To experience the full presence of God was the greatest blessing. God was always present, and they were always present for one another. Life in every sense of the word and in all aspects was truly a gift. Everything was perfect. There was no strain, stress, or struggle. They lived in paradise with each other and with God.

Imagine a life without the burden and strain of physical work as we know it. Or a life without the possibility of sickness or disease constantly looming around the corner. No cancer destroying the body, no bone-creaking arthritis disturbing your joints, no malaria, no heart disease, no mpox, and no COVID pandemic. Imagine a body that never dies and never decays. Imagine living forever not to mention being emotionally and mentally healthy. Anxiety, depression, fear, doubt, worry, and jealousy were not reality for them. Imagine living in complete harmony with the animals of the earth. You may not fully comprehend what that means or what a sweet reality it could be, but think about it. Imagine being able to walk alongside lions, tigers, bears, elephants—the beasts of the earth—without the threat of danger. Every living thing would exist harmoniously in the earth. All the elements of the earth would be in alignment with God's plan. Imagine complete love, peace, and unity amongst human beings. Rampant evil was not designed to be a part of our experience. There was no strife, murders, violence, abuse, human trafficking or persecution. No wayward children or threat of them being harmed. No separation, division, or hatred. Instead, the world was created in, sustained by, and modeled God's perfect love in every way. Everything was perfect. Adam and Eve were one with each other, and in perfect relationship with God... until the *Fall*.

In Christianity, the *Fall* is the moment in Genesis when Adam and Eve were deceived by the serpent, and they disobeyed God's command to not eat fruit from the forbidden tree (Gen. 2:15-17; 3:1-6). That one action of disobedience changed everything, and yet God did not change. This disobedience tainted Adam and Eve—they were no longer pure, they gained an awareness of the concept of good and evil, and even worse, it severed their intimate bond with God. What was once paradise became a curse upon all of creation. Everything changed, and yet God remained the same. Even in the midst of the fall, God never abandoned His creation.

God is holy and pure, which means He is generally intolerant of sin, evil, immorality, and injustice. By God's moral code, God could have destroyed Adam and Eve the moment they disobeyed Him. God could have abandoned them, and yet He didn't. Filled with shame, Adam and Eve hid themselves from God. They changed, but God remained the same relational God and sought them out (Gen. 3:9). When Adam and Eve were uncomfortable in their nakedness, it was God who took garment skins and covered them (Gen. 3:21). They changed, but God remained the same. God never "withdrew protection, support, or help from" them or "gave [them] up with the intent of never again claiming a right or interest in" humanity. In fact, throughout history He has never abandoned His creation, including you and I, through this very day. And quite frankly, He never will.

Yes, Adam's and Eve's actions corrupted and cursed creation. Because of their disobedience, every human is born under the bondage of sin and separated from God. No longer were humans allowed unrestricted access to God. We really couldn't be in full relationship with God without always having to atone (pay) for our wrongdoings. The ancient Israelites could not approach God without being destroyed unless they paid for their sins by continuously offering animal sacrifices to the

> *Does God see the depth and the pain of my abandonment issues? Does He care?*
> *(Anonymous)*

Lord. Blood from a pure animal without any blemish had to be repeatedly sacrificed. However, since humans are prone to evil, no amount of animal blood sacrifice would be enough for the remission (pardoning or cancellation) of our sins.

Everything changed. Humanity worked for, and made sacrifices for, redemption, and yet the bond between God and man remained broken. Pain, disaster, destruction, chaos, sickness, and death became the norm. But, while creation changed, our holy and relational God's desire for unrestricted relationship with His creation remained the same. God in His irrefutable love had a plan to restore order and relationship through His Son, Jesus.

Jesus is the exact manifestation of God's intention for a relationship with humanity and the opposite of all that represents abandonment. Why? Because another name by which Jesus is identified in the Bible is *Immanuel*, which in the Hebrew language means, "God with us" (Isaiah 7:14). Jesus is God in human form— the One who never sinned came as the perfect sacrifice to satisfy the requirement necessary to pay for our wrongdoings once and for all so that we could be in permanent relationship with God into eternity, never to be abandoned.[7]

God's greatest show of commitment and loyalty to humanity was when He sent His Son, thereby allowing us to be in relationship with Him and to have the opportunity for eternal life. That's the Father's heart for His creation. God loves us so much that He temporarily abandoned His only Son on the cross. One of Jesus' final words as He cried out to the Father were, "My God, my God, why have you forsaken [abandoned] me?" (Matt. 27:46). When we think about the definition of abandonment, in essence, God the Father "withdrew protection, support, and help" from His Son. Yes, God abandoned Jesus to the point of death. Jesus bore the brutality of the cross. There was no protection, support, or help. He was rejected.

Now you may be thinking, "But I thought you said God never intended for us to experience abandonment?" Yes, that's right! But God has a way of using an evil concept, like abandonment, for good. The cross[8] was a momentary abandonment that resulted in a lifetime of good. Jesus experienced the totality of abandonment on the cross so that we can have victory over abandonment forever.

The good news of the cross is Christ's ultimate victory over death and the reconciliation of humanity to God. The abandonment of Jesus was our saving grace. Much like Adam and Eve, we now have unrestricted access to God. Jesus was the ultimate sacrifice whose blood forever paid the price for our sins. Through humble and authentic repentance (a posture of being sorry or having regret for our sins) and accepting Jesus as our Lord and Savior, our broken relationship with God has been restored. God's abandonment of His own Son for the rescuing of creation is yet another strong testament to the mercy, love, and unquenchable desire of our God to be in relationship with us.

Jesus is forever with us. Acquainted with human frailty while living in His human state, Jesus is forever with us in His mercy and love as our heavenly intercessor. He is sitting at the right hand of the Father (God) in heaven interceding on your behalf. Think about that for a second. Jesus is consistently rooting for you, speaking on your behalf before the Father, and ensuring your victory. That's mind-blowing! There is no abandonment in the kingdom of God. Jesus completed His earthly assignment, transcended into heaven, now sits on His heavenly throne as our divine intercessor, and sends us the Holy Spirit as our helper here on earth.

The Holy Spirit, the third representation of God in the Holy Trinity, is yet another truth that attests to God's desire to be in relationship with us and never abandon us. In fact, Jesus said:

> *I will not leave you as orphans [comfortless, bereaved, and helpless] ... But the Helper (Comforter, Advocate, Intercessor—Counselor, Strengthener, Standby), the Holy Spirit, whom the Father will send in My name [in My place, to represent Me and act on My behalf], He will teach you all things. And He will help you remember everything that I have told you. (John 14:18, 26 AMP)*

The Holy Spirit is the Spirit of God who comforts, teaches, guides, and lovingly corrects us, making us into the people who reflect God's image and love in the earth. It is the Holy Spirit who gives us natural and supernatural revelation. Some call it *conscience*, *instinct*, *a second sense*, or *gut feeling*, but we know it to be the work of the Holy Spirit. If you have ever had knowledge about something that came from a revelatory thought or just happen to have keen insight into a situation or thing that does not come from your own effort, that's the work of the Holy Spirit. The Holy Spirit is the Spirit of Truth, guiding us into all truth (John 16:13).

It is the Holy Spirit who draws us to Christ, gives us a desire to want to know Him, and gives us understanding about who He is. The work of the Holy Spirit is evident in salvation, transforming unbelieving non-Christians into believing Christians. It is the Holy Spirit who, with the cooperation of the individual, lives within believers and transforms Christians into the best version of themselves. Through salvation, we are guaranteed the power of the Holy Spirit who empowers us to do the impossible and live out our God-given purpose. God is always with us. God has never abandoned us. God is omnipresent, meaning that He is everywhere at the same time. While the Holy Spirit is comforting someone in China, He is simultaneously guiding someone else in New York City. While He is helping someone in Russia, the Spirit of God is also helping someone in Africa. We cannot limit God's love and care for humanity. God is and will forever be our relational God.

So why then do we sometimes feel abandoned by God? Oftentimes when we have experienced traumatic situations and have experienced abandonment, it is so difficult to see God in the midst of it. Often, there is a feeling of abandonment not only by those we love but by God. But, Beloved, much like the Israelites in the Old Testament, God has made a covenant with us through His Son, Jesus, and the indwelling of the Holy Spirit to not leave us or forsake (abandon) us.[9] It was never God's intention to abandon us or for us to experience the feeling of abandonment—not in the genesis of creation and not today. Jesus loves you with the deepest and purest love you can ever imagine. Take joy in knowing you are desired and wanted by our loving God. God takes interest in you and everything concerning you. So, together let's begin the work of ditching those abandonment issues and begin living in the love and freedom Christ died for us to experience.

CHAPTER 2:

MY STORY

"But I will restore you to health and heal your wounds,"
declares the LORD. (Jeremiah 30:17 NIV)

"May May" was her name. She stood like a giant at about five foot three, sturdy, stern, giving, and nurturing. May May commanded respect. She was my maternal grandmother, the matriarch, and the CEO of what I referred to as *The Committee.* What's *The Committee*, you ask? Well, let's just say that they are my confidants—my personal board of trustees, consisting of my mother, father, maternal aunt, uncle (aunt's husband), and my maternal grandmother. *The Committee* shared, analyzed, dissected, and decided anything concerning me or any major decision.

Throughout my life, I have been tremendously blessed by who God has given me as immediate family, extended family, and friends who have become like family. I have always said my greatest currency is the village God has blessed me with. I am loved, encouraged, supported, guided, corrected, and so much more. As such, I must confess I wrestled a little bit with writing this chapter and was somewhat hesitant to write it at all. It wasn't that I was afraid to be vulnerable in sharing more of my personal story; I knew God had given me the green light to disclose it. However, in sharing, I didn't want my family to misinterpret anything or to cause shame or dishonor in any way. I didn't want them to think that I am ungrateful for all they have done for me. I am eternally thankful for them all, especially *The Committee.*

Now, you may be wondering how I ended up with a committee of parental figures and not just the average mother and father like the traditional family. Two parental figures can be challenging enough—imagine having five. And imagine how difficult it was, and sometimes still is, to navigate these relationships. I believe this may be where my issue with perceived abandonment unintentionally started.

I was probably around four years old or so when May May, who is no longer with us, suggested and ultimately decided that I should leave Jamaica, where I was born, and migrate to the United States to live with my aunt and uncle. Back in those days, no one challenged May May on anything. What she said goes, or in Jamaican terms, "She run tings" (she runs things). And so it happened, at about four years old, I went to live in New York for one year and eventually relocated to Orlando, where I spent the rest of my childhood until the age of eighteen.

I lived primarily with my aunt, uncle, and two cousins. Let me emphasize from the beginning that my aunt and uncle have always treated me as their very own. I was never made to feel like an outcast—they loved me and made it known to the world that I was their daughter. I also want to make it very clear that my biological parents were always very much in my life and certainly loved and took care of me as well. They in no way abandoned me, and in fact, my mom and dad visited me on a regular basis. My dad was already living in the US pursuing his college education. Eventually, my mother moved to the United States and joined me and the rest of the family that raised me. Additionally, because my dad and mom were no longer romantically involved, I would spend summers, some holidays, and other occasions with my father as well. I was, and still am very clear that both my parents love me.

However, despite being in a good home and having a good life, I can recall times in my earlier years when I cried and wondered why I couldn't be with my own parents all the time like other children. I suppose it would be a natural question for any child in my situation. There I was, taken away from all that I'd known and thrust into a new environment without any understanding as to why or how. My young mind could not make sense of it all; all I knew was that children were supposed to be with their parents. And yet, there I was seeing my parents for short bits of time only for them to leave again. It was a distressing dilemma, but like any child, I acclimated shortly thereafter and settled in well.

I had the best upbringing and childhood. I was loved by so many people—*The Committee* being my main supporters. I don't know if there is such a thing as being overloved, but if there is,

I think I fit the description. I was stifled with love and lived in an extreme opposite reality from a child who is abandoned or neglected. I could not imagine my life any differently. In fact, I don't know who I would be if things were different. I thank God for all my experiences. I am the person that I am today because of this specific pathway in my journey.

However, life began to unravel when I crossed paths with Dr. Rob Reimer in seminary and was exposed to some of his teachings, as well as other great scholars who I met during my seminary experience—all of whom are attuned to and skilled in emotional soul trauma and healing. It was then I realized I was carrying some hidden emotional wounds that, to my surprise, related to my childhood. It was when I fully submerged myself into Dr. Reimer's Soul Care teachings and ministry process that God gave me the revelation that I was struggling with abandonment issues. I was so confused! My first thought was, "Me? I'm struggling with abandonment? But how?"

> They say that abandonment is a wound that never heals. I say only that an abandoned child never forgets.
> (Mario Balotelli, Professional Football Player)

Consciously, I never felt my parents deserted me at all and I never saw myself as abandoned. The thought never crossed my mind nor do I hold any resentment for what happened. I knew the decision for me to move to America was made with the best intention of affording me the opportunity of a better life. Yet, when I began to look deeper, I found myself checking the boxes that matched the characteristic traits of someone with abandonment issues—distrustful of everyone, a people-pleaser, choosing unhealthy romantic relationships, and so much more. When I talked with Dr. Reimer, he confirmed that I had abandonment issues and helped me further understand why I had this struggle and why I behaved the way I did. The revelation that I was living as one abandoned—although I was not—was alarming.

One of the things that Dr. Reimer helped me understand was that my childhood mind could not fully process my experience of not being raised by my parents in a traditional home. I was too young to truly rationalize all that was happening. I didn't have the emotional development to grieve the loss of not being with my parents regularly, so I simply coped and adapted to my new normal. But the effects of that loss subconsciously manifested in different ways in my life because those childhood feelings and confusion were never addressed.

Somewhere in the very early years of my transition to my new American life, I may have somehow felt abandoned. But because I never processed it, it surfaced in other ways in my adolescent and adult years instead. Unprocessed issues of the soul—whether they are abandonment, neglect, abuse, and so much more—always manifest in unhealthy behavioral patterns in one form or another. Despite having a great childhood, being loved by all my parental figures, and accomplishing all I had in my adult life, God began to show me through Soul Care the unhealthy mindset, behavior patterns, and energy that I embodied related to the bondage of abandonment issues. I was so grateful for this revelation because the first step to healing is awareness. My newfound understanding was the beginning of a long, beautiful, and ongoing journey to healing and freedom.

SECTION 2

ROOT CAUSES OF ABANDONMENT ISSUES

CHAPTER 3:

ROOT CAUSES OF ABANDONMENT

The Lord himself goes before you and will be with you; he will never leave you nor forsake you. Do not be afraid; do not be discouraged. (Deuteronomy 31:8 NIV)

Living a life of freedom, fullness, and fulfillment requires us to address the root causes of abandonment issues. There are so many scenarios and situations that could lead to one experiencing the effects of abandonment, but I wanted to highlight some common circumstances that most people encounter. This is in no way a comprehensive list, and you may not be able to identify with any of the scenarios listed. However, I do hope that as you read, you will gain some insight into your own unique circumstances.

PERCEIVED ABANDONMENT

Perceived abandonment occurs when a person exhibits abandonment issues when objectively they have not been abandoned. At some point in their life, this individual has internalized the notion that they have been abandoned. One may experience this abandonment for the following reasons:

- **Unconventional Family Dynamics**

  Being raised by nonbiological parents is not unique to me. It is common in many cultures around the world and even considered the norm for children to be raised by extended family and even close family friends. As a Jamaican, I know it is especially common in Caribbean culture. I personally know of friends, aunts, uncles, and cousins who were raised by their grandparents or other relatives. The circumstances leading to this family dynamic vary, but most commonly, children are partially raised with nonparental family members for economic reasons.

  A parent or parents in search of better opportunities and financial stability for their children may find themselves having to relocate temporarily and sometimes even permanently. When this occurs, the child sees their parents infrequently, but they are still very much involved in the child's life from a distance. This relocation may be as simple as moving from a rural, underdeveloped area to a more developed, urbanized city in the same region. Or it may be as complex as migrating to an entirely new country altogether. The migration of the parent does not equate to the child being abandoned in the real and objective sense of the word. These parents did not "withdraw protection, support, or help from" or "give up with the intent of never again claiming a right or interest in" their child or children. To the contrary, the decision to leave the child was one that was grounded in love and concern for the child's future well-being.

Yet, despite good intentions, these decisions are difficult for both the parent and child, and they often result in unpredicted and undeniable negative long-term effects for both. Even with admirable motives, I would venture to say that most parents are not fully aware of the emotional damage leaving their child may cause. Again,

> *I had to get in touch with the source, I had to go back into my abandonment issues with my mother, I had to go into issues with my father I hadn't even looked at before.*
> *(Kenny Loggins, American Singer and Guitarist)*

while the child was not abandoned in the true sense of the word, over time, he or she may exhibit signs of abandonment issues due to this separation and their inability to process the emotions associated with their unconventional family dynamics.

- **Unhealthy Attachment**

  Perceived abandonment may occur when children with unhealthy attachments grow to become adults who develop

27

abandonment issues and separation anxiety disorder (SAD).

Separation anxiety is a regular part of childhood development in infants and young children. It begins between ages of six to twelve months and usually resolves by the age of three (around preschool level). It is common and developmentally normal for a child to display some level of worry about caregivers leaving them. A child with normal separation anxiety may demonstrate:

- "A reluctance to leave their caregiver."
- "Crying or tantrums when a caregiver leaves the room."
- "Clinging or crying, especially in new situations."
- "Awakening/crying at night although in the past they have slept through the night."
- "Refusal to go to sleep without a parent nearby."
- "Anxiety about going to daycare or school."[10]

However, separation anxiety—which is normal and expected in childhood development—is not to be confused with SAD. SAD is a classified mental health disease and is defined as:

Diagnosis assigned to individuals who have an unusually strong fear or anxiety to separating from people they feel a strong attachment to. The diagnosis is given only when the distress associated with separation is unusual for an individual's developmental level, is prolonged and severe. The need to stay in close proximity to caretakers can make it difficult for children with this disorder to go to school, stay at friends houses or be in a room by themselves. In adults it can make normal developmental activities like moving away from home, getting married or being an independent person very difficult.[11]

According to the Diagnostic and Statistical Manual of Mental Disorders 5 (DSM-5), a diagnosis of SAD is diagnosed in individuals who meet the following criteria:[12]

1) Excess or developmentally inappropriate fear or anxiety about separation from whom the individual is attached to as shown by exhibiting at least three of the following:

   a. "Recurrent excessive distress when anticipating or experiencing separation from home or from major attachment figures."

   b. "Persistent and excessive worry about losing major attachment figures or about possible harm to them, such as illness, injury, disasters, or death."

   c. "Persistent and excessive worry about experiencing an untoward event (e.g., getting lost, being kidnapped, having an accident, becoming ill) that causes separation from a major attachment figure."

d. "Persistent reluctance or refusal to go out, away from home, to school, to work, or elsewhere because of fear of separation."

e. "Persistent and excessive fear of or reluctance about being alone or without major attachment figures at home or in other settings."

f. "Persistent reluctance or refusal to sleep away from home or to go to sleep without being near a major attachment figure."

2) "Symptoms persist for a minimum of four weeks."

3) "The symptoms or disturbance are not explained and are not a result of another mental health disorder such as autism spectrum disorder, delusion or hallucinations in psychotic disorder, agoraphobia, and other anxiety disorders."

It is this SAD, if not dealt with, that has the potential to create abandonment issues. Even with a history of love and support, a child with abandonment issues may perceive prolonged absence as abandonment and associate it with being unloved or unwanted. This child grows to become an adult who views life and relationships from the lens of rejection. Separation experiences then trigger the notion of being unloved, undesirable, and even abandoned. However, is this individual actually abandoned? Absolutely not.

Yet they perceive themselves as repeatedly abandoned, suffer from abandonment issues, and regularly exhibit unhealthy behavioral patterns, including repeated participation in dysfunctional relationships.

TRUE ABANDONMENT

Now while there is perceived abandonment, there is also true abandonment. A person who experiences true abandonment is one who has, in reality, been left behind and neglected, and has minimal to no communication, connection, or involvement with the person who has left them. This individual (the abandonee) has been neglected in many ways including, but not limited to, physically, financially, and emotionally. In other words, the abandoner has truly "withdraw[n] protection, support, or help from" or has "give[n] up with the intent of never again claiming a right or interest in" the abandonee. Similar to perceived abandonment, people who experience true abandonment may exhibit signs of SAD and various forms of unhealthy emotions and dysfunctional behaviors. Some of the most prevalent root causes of true abandonment are:

- **Abandonment Through Formal and Informal Adoption:**

  When we think about true abandonment, one of the most obvious causes that comes to mind is adoption— children whose parents gave up their parental rights and responsibility to another. This child is abandoned by their parents and given up for adoption, placed in the foster care system, or given over to another caretaker (including informal adoption through extended family and friends).

A parent may willingly relinquish their parental rights because they are self-aware enough to recognize their flaws and in humility make the choice to give their child a better opportunity apart from themselves. This parent has accepted that perhaps they are irresponsible, negligent, abusive, suffering from significant mental health disease, struggling with unhealthy addictions, financially unfit, or limited in some capacity that deems them as unfit parents. Thus they have come to the conclusion that it would be in the child's best interest to be placed with more stable or capable parental figures. Of note there are also cases where the parents must involuntarily relinquish care of the child not based on their own choice, but as the states deems the parents unfit the child is taken away by force–still putting the child at risk of later suffering abandonment issues.

In addition, a parent may abandon their child through adoption simply because of selfish reasons. This parent finds parenthood to be burdensome and distracting. Thus, in an effort to regain their simplified, self-absorbed life, they give up their responsibilities as a caregiver.

It is evident there are several reasons a child may experience abandonment through formal or informal adoption. Despite some decisions being grounded in the right motives and good reasons, the reality is that children who have been abandoned through adoption run the risk of developing abandonment issues that affect them throughout their lives.

- **Abandonment in Single-Parent Households**

Currently the United States demonstrates the world's highest rate of children living in single parent households. This fact is based on a Pew Research Study of 130 countries and territories looking at single parent living arrangements. Astoundingly, "almost a quarter of U.S. children under the age of 18 live with one parent and no other adults (23%)," which is three times the rate of children living in single-parent households around the world (7%).[13] Released on December 12, 2019, this report speaks to a very common phenomenon in America in recent years.

It is important to note here that single-parent households do not equate to abandonment. There are many people who have been raised in single-parent households where there is a healthy co-parenting arrangement and both parents are involved in the care of their children. In essence, this child is not considered abandoned as he or she has the support and care of both parents, albeit in separate home settings. However, when one parent has left and is not present for the child in any capacity, this is considered true abandonment. Although loved and cared for by one parent, the absence of the other increases the chances of this child experiencing abandonment issues.

- **Abandonment By Neglect**

  When we think about abandonment by neglect, there are two forms that come to mind: material and emotional.

  - *Material neglect* is the failure to provide or to intentionally withhold basic needs from a child and/or adult. If necessities such as food, education, shelter, clothing, and access to medical care are being withheld from an individual, later development of abandonment issues is common.

  - *Emotional neglect* is the absence or withdrawal of emotional support and care for a child and/or adult.

    - *Childhood Emotional Neglect:* Children thrive, develop well, and have a healthy sense of self and purpose when they are nurtured, guided, and encouraged by parental figures and loved ones. This healthy development happens when there are positive interactions and affections such as words of affirmation, kisses, hugs, and playfulness within the home. However, since love is denoted in varying ways, and oftentimes determined by cultural norms, a child may still develop a healthy sense of self in the absence of frequently hearing "I love you" or experiencing physical affection. For instance, I personally did not grow up with frequent physical acts of affection, the cultural norm in Caribbean households. However, my parents' very palpable protectiveness, concern for my well-being, intentionality in exposing me to different opportunities, encouragement, praise, provision, and even discipline were evidence of their care and love for me. It is to be noted that provision is a huge love language in many cultures, one that should be recognized and validated. Love and care, in whichever way they are communicated, are important to the emotional well-being of the child.

However, childhood emotional neglect that leads to the feeling of true abandonment happens in environments where one or both parents are cold, unaffectionate, emotionally detached, overly critical, angry, or condemning. The child may feel unloved and blame themselves for being ignored. Additionally, children may feel neglectful abandonment in households where there is abuse of any sort, addictions to substances like drugs and alcohol, mental health disease, unresolved hurts or trauma, workaholism, and/

or favoritism of one child over another. All of these circumstances may lead to abandonment issues later in life.

○ *Adulthood Emotional Neglect:* Adult emotional neglect occurs when a loved one—inclusive of a spouse, romantic partner, sibling, friend, extended family, and even colleague—is physically present yet emotionally absent. This loved one is cold, distant, unaffectionate, uncommunicative, overly critical, discouraging, and overall emotionally detached.

In adults, emotional neglect quite often leads to physical neglect (abandonment). Couples who have the unfortunate experience of facing separation or divorce are concrete examples of both emotional and physical abandonment. One marital partner may become less emotionally involved by exhibiting complete emotional detachment or even by focusing their emotional energy on an outside person (as in the case of infidelity). Consequently, these actions may eventually lead to a physical withdrawal of the neglectful spouse from the martial union. When the party who is on the receiving end of the neglect is faced with the reality of a broken marital covenant that ends in separation or divorce from an intertwined life with their spouse, not only is it deeply painful but may result in the development of abandonment issues as they are left to deal with the loss

Finally, adults in platonic friendships as well as committed nonmarital relationships run the risk of experiencing abandonment issues when one party withdraws themselves emotionally and physically from the relationship. Severed bonds and a violation in the connection between parties may leave an individual feeling rejected and abandoned.

The above-mentioned scenarios are only a few root causes of abandonment issues. There are a myriad of circumstances that may lead to us experiencing perceived or true abandonment. Whatever the cause, the goal is not to remain stuck but to be healed, delivered, and set free from the burden of abandonment issues.

As you begin your journey toward a better self, take the time to reflect on how you may have experienced abandonment. Ask yourself the following questions:

- *Was it true abandonment or perceived abandonment?*
- *Did it stem from childhood, or did it happen in adulthood?*
- *Who do you know or believe abandoned you?*
- *Have you acknowledged, processed, and healed from abandonment, or is this your first step in recognizing and confronting it?*

I fully recognize that it may be painful to address some of these questions. Facing your issues of abandonment can be a long and painful process, so extend yourself grace. However, acknowledgment of the root causes is the first step to breakthrough. I have faith you can do it. You can overcome abandonment issues and live in the victory and freedom you deserve.

CHAPTER 4:

ABANDONMENT AND IDENTITY

So God created mankind in his own image, in the image of God he created them; male and female he created them.
(Genesis. 1:27 NIV)

At the root of abandonment issues is an identity problem. That identity problem can stem from being abandoned. In other words, perceived or true abandonment leads to an identity problem, which then leads to abandonment issues. Let's talk about these complex dynamics in more detail. Your identity is what sets you apart from anyone or anything else on the earth. It is what makes each one of us a beautifully unique asset to this world and to those we encounter. Identity encompasses every aspect of your life. Therefore, whenever there is a breach in the formation of one's identity, a myriad of issues, including abandonment issues, become the norm.

Identity may be defined as "who you are, the way you think about yourself, the way you are viewed by the world and the characteristics that define you."[14] I love this definition because it is a reminder that one's identity plays a key role in every aspect of one's life. The way you are viewed by the world and the characteristics that define you are based on certain accepted societal rules, norms, and standard practices. Aspects of our lives such as gender, race, ethnicity, profession, career, level of achievement, intellect, eye color, body build, hair texture, and so on are defined by certain societal definitions and protocols. However, despite society's standards, having a strong sense of identity is rooted in recognizing that who you are and the characteristics that define you are a powerful combination of everything that makes you uniquely you.

The way we think about ourselves is so vitally important. A positive self-view will keep us afloat when we don't meet the approval and standards of others. It is natural to place a heavy weight on how the world and those we value view us. We all want the approval of others, but our own self-perspective is foundational to a healthy sense of self and often determines how we respond to another person's perspective of us. As adults, accepting society's definition of who we are while not having a healthy or truthful view of ourselves results in a fractured soul. However, paradoxically, our identity—who we think we are and how we view ourselves—is largely shaped by other people in our earlier years of life. These perspectives of ourselves, whether right or wrong, have a major impact on how we see ourselves even in adulthood.

According to experts in child development, during the first eleven years of life, our sense of self primarily develops from what

ABANDONMENT AND IDENTITY

other people tell us. In other words, we do not have our own sense of self in the first decade of our lives. In that first decade, our identity is shaped by the words, care, love, actions, and concern of important authority figures. These key individuals may be parents, guardians, siblings, extended family members, teachers, and even religious leaders. When we are surrounded by encouragement and validation, we develop a healthier view of self. Positive words and actions that affirm our existence, highlight us as special, and encourage us when we are doing something well or right are all pivotal to the development of a healthy self-identity. When love is radiated in spite of wrongdoing, weakness, or failure, a healthy self-acceptance develops.

However, when our childhood is marred by such factors as the absence of parental figures, key role models, and loved ones or afflicted by other realities such as instability or failure to have important needs met (like safety, comfort, provision, boundaries, discipline, and overall normalcy), then a skewed sense of being is formed—one that dictates how we show up in adulthood. As such, we can surmise that children with healthy identities become adults with healthy identities. And by the same token, children with unhealthy identities become adults with unhealthy identities, which then opens the door to abandonment issues.

Adults with a solid sense of identity are those who have a balanced dose of self-love, self-esteem, and self-validation. They recognize their strengths, talents, and gifts and can comfortably acknowledge that they have something to contribute to the world.

They are not over-reliant on outside validation for self-acceptance or approval. They do not ask for permission to do well or be great. They don't rely on the words of others to see the beauty of who they are. They recognize that when God created the universe and said it was "very good" (Gen. 1:31), they are included in that definition of what is good. The core of who they are is *good* not because they are perfect but because God says His creation is good—even with flaws, faults, and shortcomings. For this individual, it is not about being pompous, egotistical, or prideful. They are very much aware that they are flawed. But they recognize there is always a chance for healing, positive change, growth, and transformation. They believe that there is always an opportunity for the Lord to redeem and change those areas in their life that are not in line with who they were created to be.

> *After spending much of my life trying to become who I thought people wanted me to be, I question if I really ever knew who I was.*

In contrast, adults who do not have a healthy sense of identity may develop abandonment issues and struggle with low self-esteem, lack of self-confidence, and a low self-worth. Abandonment issues may cause one to feel out of place and not accepted, much like an orphan. There is a sense or feeling of not belonging. Consequently, individuals whose abandonment issues are rooted in an unhealthy view of self—often resulting in an identity crisis—may also develop unhealthy behavior patterns including, but not limited to: performance-based living, people-pleasing, control issues, and living the false self. In his book *Soul Care*, Dr. Reimer describes these behaviors as *unhealthy core lies* that we believe about our identity. He discusses at length how they relate to poor soul health.[15] Let's look more closely at these lies and their accompanying dysfunctional behaviors as they relate to abandonment issues.

PERFORMANCE

The performance lie is the thought that one's value is dependent on how well one performs or does anything in life. If you do something well, you've rightfully earned the validation or affirmation you are seeking. But if you fail or fall short, you are not deemed as worthy. As Dr. Reimer rightfully points out, society often reinforces this kind of lie, maybe not intentionally, but it is naturally reinforced. Think about it. From a young age, we are rewarded and praised when we do well, which encourages us to want to work harder to earn that positive affirmation. This behavior and reward cycle is often carried over into adulthood and is a natural part of human behavior.

Generally, there is nothing innately wrong with rewarding positive behaviors or achievements. The problem comes when we equate our identity primarily with success. When you develop the mindset that your worth, value, or right to receive love is based on excelling, you bear the exhausting challenge of always trying to meet the expectations you believe others are placing on you and those that you've internally placed on yourself. Performers tend to be perfectionists and have perfectionist tendencies. In anything they do, they are not satisfied until it is perfect in their own mind. Imagine carrying this type of weight all the time. As someone who has lived it, believe me, it is draining. Yet people who are plagued with abandonment syndrome live this reality.

Food For Thought:

- *Can you think of some areas where you attach your worth to how well you perform (i.e., in school, work/profession/job title, having certain gifts or skills)?*
- *Can you identify the root of this performance behavior?*
- *How does performing benefit you?*

PEOPLE-PLEASING

Along the same path of the performance lie is people-pleasing. People pleasers extend themselves to gain the approval of others to feel a sense of worth and acceptance. Going beyond the norm of healthy compromise, pleasers put others before themselves to the point of sacrificing their own comfort in an ongoing basis. In the name of altruism and love, there is nothing innately wrong with putting others first. God's second greatest commandment is to love our neighbors as we love ourselves (Mark 12:31). However, it becomes pathologic when satisfying others is our default.

People pleasers often have a hard time telling people *no* and consent to doing things that they often resent doing later. Commonly, they take on too much, end up forgoing their own desires just to suit other people, and have the unhealthy habit of saying *yes* to things even when not sincere. For example, as a working mother, you may have had a long day at work. You finally cooked dinner, fed the kids, and put them to sleep. The plan is to catch up on some email and go directly to bed. However, at 10 p.m. the phone rings, and it is a friend who you admire and value. This friend needs help with a project, and they need help immediately. Although all you want to do is rest after a long day, because you are a people pleaser, you ignore your own desires and consent to assisting. This help is not purely out of kindness, but to please and pacify the person you hold in high esteem. Saying yes is a means of gaining approval and avoiding loss of the friendship (i.e., preventing abandonment).

If you are unable to relate to the above scenario, perhaps instead of a working mother, you are a man whose work supervisor unfairly passes their responsibilities to you while receiving compensation and taking the credit for the work you have done. Instead of speaking up against this unjust behavior, the people pleaser within you continues to do the work, believing that you will gain favor with the boss. Or perhaps you're a spouse or partner who constantly yields to the demands of your significant other, forgoing your own wants and needs while never voicing your *no*. Your uncompromising *yes* to your partner is a result of your fear of them abandoning you. However, if not dealt with, bitterness, anger, and resentment will build up over time and eventually lead to strain in the relationship.

I can honestly say that people-pleasing has been a constant challenge in my own life. As a person who is a natural helper, it was especially hard to say no to family and friends. I secretly developed resentment of people who constantly burdened me with their crises and who were particularly draining because they knew I would always put their needs before my own. I routinely allowed people to make their crisis my crisis. But I have come a far way in overcoming this behavior.

As I healed from my abandonment issues, I recognized I could not blame anyone but myself. It was within my power to say no. I realized that I was not obligated to do anything to gain the approval of anyone. Saying *no*, setting boundaries, and making myself a priority helped to bring balance as a nurturer. When I let go of people-pleasing, I became more available to others in a healthy way, while also being available to myself. I can now be more fully present for others from a pure and genuine emotional place.

Can you relate? You may know what it's like to place your needs on the back burner while prioritizing the needs of others. You may know what it's like to live with the fear of abandonment, and so you do everything to please everyone around except yourself. You don't have to continue to live the people-pleasing lie. Beloved, it's time to be healed and delivered from the strain of people-pleasing.

ABANDONMENT AND IDENTITY

Food For Thought:

- *In what ways have you been a people pleaser?*
- *Who are the people you strive to please the most and why?*
- *Identify the underlying fears that cause you to exhibit the behavior (i.e., fear of losing the relationship, not being loved).*

CONTROL

Controlling behavior is yet another major area of struggle for those who suffer from abandonment issues. To understand the reasoning behind control issues in abandoned individuals, we must first recognize that being abandoned by another person is something we cannot control. We cannot force anyone to stay in our lives or support, help, or claim interest in us. But, most notably in close relationships, the abandonee will strive to be in control to avoid being left again. Neediness, the tendency to be overly clingy, and a lack of respect for healthy boundaries are commonly seen.

Yet controlling tendencies are not restricted to close relationships. As a measure of security, we may attempt to control the actions of even outside people in our lives for our benefit and struggle in areas where we are not in control. For instance, for the abandoned person, group collaboration can be quite challenging. We often have a hard time delegating responsibilities without micromanaging or being overly critical. Again, we want to facilitate the best outcome for ourselves, and in our mind, that cannot happen unless we are fully involved and in control. Having control issues leads to increased stress, anger, anxiety, and resentment when faced with situations where we lack control.

In my personal experience, anger is the emotion that often surfaced when I was not in control. If I was a victim of any injustice—no matter how trivial—and there was no apology or justice given for the wrong done to me, anger reared its ugly head. My anger primarily stemmed from my inability to force the offending party to right their wrong. If a patient or a loved one was engaging in destructive behavior, I was both anxious and angry because they would not make better choices. If certain things were not done in a particular way, you guessed it: irritability and agitation overtook me. At times, I displayed my anger outwardly, yet just as frequently, I seethed inwardly as well.

However, since learning to relinquish that constant need for control and accepting that I am powerless to change anyone but myself, my life is more peaceful. I've come to the realization that people can only change if they choose to change. I've learned to be more flexible and adaptable in even the most challenging circumstances. It continues to be a work in progress, but I have made great strides in overcoming control issues. Needless to say, the need for control is a significant interference in the lives of people with abandonment issues.

ABANDONMENT AND IDENTITY

Food for Thought:

- *Based on the reading, do you identify as someone with control issues?*
- *Can you identify specific situations or circumstances where you more forcefully try to exert control?*
- *What emotions do you often experience when you are not in control?*

FALSE SELF

Behind every mask is a true face. Behind every falsity is the truth. The concept of the false self is a theory that is primarily credited to pediatrician and psychoanalyst Dr. David Winnicott and one that shows up overwhelmingly in people with abandonment issues. The false self is an artificial persona, a protective mechanism that people typically create in their early childhood to prevent developmental trauma, shock, and stress in close relationships. According to Winnicott, in as early as infancy, individuals learn that certain behaviors foster more positive interactions with their parents while also lessening the parent's fear and anxieties. Hence, the child will then bury their natural spontaneous behaviors and replace them with behaviors that yield a favorable parental response.[16] This

49

persona carries over into adulthood to gain approval in a variety of spaces including our personal and professional lives.

As a mask, the false self is used to showcase what society deems as acceptable behavior. It is often a mechanism to hide guilt, shame, and vulnerabilities. It is the persona we want the world to see masquerading as a decoy to hide the parts of us we detest. The false self appears poised, put together, joyful, confident, wise, in control, and overall stable. But in extreme cases, those who live a false self may be left feeling dead and empty inside. What is particularly troubling about the false self is that it can lead to stifling of the true self. According to Winnicott, the true self is associated with authenticity, spontaneity, and a very real and fulfilling sense of being alive. The true self—the good, the bad, and the ugly—is the vulnerable self that lives freely in its truth. But under the domination of the false self, the true self may be eclipsed and eventually fail to thrive.

Now I must concede that a healthy false self, or what I would call a *corrected self*, is necessary. For instance, if I'm having a bad day or I'm in a bad mood, for the sake of keeping my job, it would be unwise to let *irritable Tanesha* come forward unrestricted and unrestrained. Touching the lives of others requires the right attitude, even when I may not feel inwardly the positivity I project outwardly. In the name of love, respect, morality, protocol, and even etiquette, moments of presenting a false self may be prudent. The problem, however, is when we become so dependent on living the false self that we begin to deny our real selves. Living the false self comes at the expense of losing our authentically true self. Not only does it hinder the unique parts of who we are while stifling our gifts, talents, and abilities, but it also prevents us from dealing with those parts of ourselves that need healing—the ugly parts of us that we all carry.

The false self is often an integral defense mechanism for people afflicted with abandonment. Yet the world is a better place when you live who you are. There is joy and freedom in being true to yourself! Let's begin to dismantle the false self as a major stride in our journey to healing and wholeness.

Food For Thought:

- *Do an honest reflection of yourself—do you have a false self?*
- *What flaws and vulnerabilities are you trying to hide behind this false self?*
- *What are some characteristics of your false self? In other words, what does your false self look like to the world?*
- *What are some characteristics of your true self, both good and bad?*

SECTION 3

EFFECTS OF ABANDONMENT ISSUES

CHAPTER 5:

SHAME

Do not be afraid; you will not be put to shame. Do not fear disgrace; you will not be humiliated. You will forget the shame of your youth and remember no more the reproach of your widowhood.
(Isaiah 54:4 NIV)

Like me, I'm sure you can recall one or several moments where you have experienced the weighty embarrassment of shame. Shame is a very real part of the human experience and a very common struggle for those of us with abandonment issues. Yet similar to how it was never God's intention in His initial design for us to experience abandonment, it was never His intent for us to experience the brokenness of shame.

THEORY FOR THE ORIGIN OF SHAME VS. GOD'S INTENTION

Recalling the book of Genesis, remember that when God created the universe, He saw it all as good (Gen. 1:31). The animals, plant life, seas, land, sun, moon, stars, human beings—He saw it all as good. He delighted in what He made. He delights in you and me. You bring God joy. Can you imagine that? You make God smile. He created us, He created you and me, to be in a healthy relationship with Him. He longs to shower you with His love, and He in turn desires you to love Him and know Him intimately.

God was never ashamed of us. Shame came into the equation through Adam and Eve. Not only did disobeying God bring sin into the world and a curse on creation, but it also introduced the weight of shame, a common emotion that plagues many of us today. The Bible says when Adam and Eve ate the apple, their eyes were opened, and they became aware that they were naked. And they, in shame, hid and covered their nakedness (Gen. 3:7, 10).

Please note: they were naked all the time. However, the knowledge and awareness of their nakedness that came with eating from that tree made them feel shame—a shame that neither they, you, nor I were ever supposed to feel.

GUILT VS. TOXIC SHAME

Those of us who deal with abandonment experience extraordinary amounts of shame. That shame is rooted in thinking you are not good enough. That somehow it is your fault that you were rejected or not accepted by that family member, boyfriend, girlfriend, or friend. It's the scenario in your imagination that Dad left and never returned because maybe you were too naughty, not lovable, or not worthy of a father's love. It's experiencing a failed marriage or dating relationship and feeling the weight of imaginary eyes scrutinizing you. It's feeling the sting of hurt when a friend suddenly turns on you and ends the friendship for no apparent reason.

Oh, we have all experienced shame in our lives. However, it is important to distinguish between guilt and shame. They may appear similar but there is a difference. Guilt is behavior-related, while shame is identity-related.

A deep-seated feeling of unworthiness and the constant awareness of being flawed lies central to the back-breaking, soul-shattering, spirit-draining power and oppression of shame . . . a power we must overcome.

Guilt: Guilt is feeling bad about your behavior. It assumes something is wrong with your *actions or what you've done,* but overall, you still have a positive view of yourself.

Shame: Contrary to guilt, shame takes the self-condemning perspective that there is *something wrong with you as a person.* That you are worthless, deeply flawed, and not good. Shame is rooted in a lack of self-love and self-validation. Consequently, there are two main types of shame: ordinary shame and toxic shame.

- *Ordinary Shame*: In a heightened moment, you may feel ordinary shame as a regular part of the human experience. Ordinary shame is a negative self-view that occurs momentarily in a particular circumstance, but over time, that negative perspective resolves. Ordinary shame is a temporary feeling.

- ***Toxic Shame:*** Toxic shame, however, is a trait that people associate with their own identity. It has become a part of who you are and is an ongoing experience. It is that constant feeling and inward self-perspective of unworthiness.[17] Toxic shame is a dysfunctional, life-crushing shame that many people with abandonment syndrome experience as they live in the bondage of self-condemnation.

The phrase *hang your head in shame* so powerfully gives a visual of how shame affects us. The weight of shame not only burdens you and steals your peace, but it literally makes it difficult to lift your head and walk in the pride, confidence, and dignity that come with healthy self-love and self-acceptance.

Before I had a significant breakthrough in my healing journey, I remember finding difficulty in holding my head high and looking people in the eye because of a variety of reasons for shame. Because of the norm of people of Caribbean culture being overly critical and Jamaicans being extremely so, I was overly conscious of my appearance. One moment it was noted that I was too skinny, but the minute I put on a few pounds, I was getting fat. I felt shame. After experiencing a failed marriage in my twenties and going through a string of bad relationships, I felt shame. Because I wasn't flashy enough, I suppose, or I didn't "look like a doctor" as vocalized by some people around me, I felt ashamed. Being labeled as weird because I didn't always act like or move like the crowd caused me to feel shame. These were some of the things that caused me to be weighed down by shame.

But I'm here to tell you as someone who has overcome toxic shame that God wants you to be free from all unhealthy shame. You were not created to be in bondage to shame of any kind. You are worthy of God's love. As an initial step in overcoming shame and finding freedom, choose today to embrace the truth that you are loved, accepted, and wanted. Meditate on this phrase and say, "I am God's beloved." You are not abandoned. You are worthy! There is no shame in you.

Food For Thought:

- *In what areas are you currently experiencing shame?*
- *Can you specifically identify areas of shame that come from early childhood or may be related to the actions of family or loved ones?*
- *What are some condemning thoughts or phrases that repeatedly come to your mind and cause you to feel shame?*
- *Where or who do those phrases come from?*

CHAPTER 6:

FEAR AND ANXIETY

*So do not fear, for I am with you; do not be dismayed, for
I am your God. I will strengthen you and help you;
I will uphold you with my righteous right hand.
(Isaiah 41:10 NIV)*

Fear and anxiety are two pervasive emotional disturbances that are always associated with abandonment issues. I find myself intrigued by superstar gospel artist Kirk Franklin's song called "Hello Fear." In the song, Kirk masterfully depicts the emotion of fear as a person he has an unhealthy, toxic relationship with and he must break ties with. Art truly and accurately depicts life in that many of us have allowed fear to dominate our lives and rob us of our joy, peace, fulfillment, and purpose.

God knew fear was a very real struggle in the human experience; hence, in anticipation of our struggle, this command and encouragement of not fearing is repeatedly reinforced throughout the biblical canon. Fear has stifled and kept many from living out the dreams and purpose they were destined to live. There are books that have never been written, businesses never started, ideas never developed, companies never formed, jobs never attained, and lives never impacted because of fear.

Not surprisingly, with fear commonly comes anxiety, and these two vices often work in tandem to wreak havoc in our lives. At the time this book is being written, anxiety has soared to take its place as the number one mental health disease in the United States, affecting 40 million adults (19.1% of the population) aged 18 years and older.[18] Far from being straightforward, anxiety is a complex disease where several contributing factors may be at play including genetics, personality, brain chemistry and life events. Additionally, in some Christian circles, it is believed that anxiety may manifest because of spiritual factors as well.

> *In my own experience fear was always lurking close by persistent, powerful, pervasive and unrelenting in its intention to destroy who God designed me to be.*

Whatever the cause, I love how my former seminary professor Dr. Mike Plunket, pastor of Risen King Church in New City, NY, gives accurate insight when he says, *anxiety is a voice from hell that incites worry and negative feelings over a reality that may never happen.* How much time do we waste in our lives worrying about possible outcomes that may never happen? We lose sleep, live in tension, and literally make ourselves sick over *what if, maybe*, and things that may never come to pass or that we cannot control. Fear and anxiety can even take a physical toll on the body as they both have been linked to increased risks of heart attack, stroke, and stomach ulcers. In far-reaching ways, fear is a primary destroyer of our joy, peace, and freedom that limits our potential and gravely lessens our quality of life.

People who are plagued by abandonment issues often experience a unique associated fear called the fear of abandonment, which is an intense fear of losing someone you love. The fear of abandonment is considered a type of anxiety, and I would surmise that most people with abandonment issues experience this unique type of fear in varying degrees. Believed to have origins in childhood, the fear of abandonment may stem from "1) interruptions in the normal development of certain cognitive and emotional capacities, 2) challenges with past relationships and 3) [enduring] other problematic social and life experiences" in our younger, formative years.[19] In other words, unhealthy interferences in the development of a child's ability to think, reason, or focus, or experiencing ongoing childhood trauma and difficult relationships can lead to fear of abandonment that carries over into adulthood. Again, think of persistent parental absence in the home or emotional neglect as early factors that may later lead to deep-rooted fears of losing loved ones. Consequently, people with abandonment syndrome and the fear of abandonment may exhibit some of the following behaviors:[20]

"Form quick attachments—even to unavailable partners or relationships;"

"Fail to fully commit, few long-term relationships;"

"Move on quickly just to ensure less attachment;"

"Aim to please;"

"Engage in unwanted sex (this is common in women);"

"Stay in unhealthy relationships;"

"Struggle with being hard to please and nitpicky;"

"Have difficulty experiencing emotional intimacy;"

"Feel insecure and unworthy of love;"

"Find it hard to trust people;"

"Are often jealous of everyone they meet."

"Experience intense feelings of separation anxiety;"

"Have feelings of general anxiety and depression;"

"Tend to overthink things and work hard to figure out hidden meanings;"

"Are hypersensitive to criticism;"

"Contain repressed anger and control issues;"

"Engage in self-blame frequently."

If you are dealing with abandonment, you may not experience all these symptoms, but it is common for people to experience several. The ones that have been prominent in my own life were people-pleasing, distrust of others, self-blame, not holding others accountable for wrong-doings, staying in unhealthy relationships, and struggling with repressed anger and control issues.

Upon close inspection, you may notice the running themes among these symptoms are: 1) lack of self-love 2) people-pleasing 3) unhealthy attachment styles and 4) excessive defense mechanisms—all of which are driven by fear.

Throughout this book, we have already discussed the lack of self-love and the propensity for people-pleasing in those with abandonment issues. We've talked about how abandonment weaves the false narrative that you are not worthy and you carry little to no value. It says everyone else is far superior to you and, to fit in, you must earn your place. In your mind, to gain love, affection, and respect from those you admire or hold dear, you must earn it. If you are an abandoned person, you are not pleased unless the object of your affection is pleased. Your joy and worth stem from the approval and validation of an outside source and not from within.

However, beyond people-pleasing and lacking self-love, to live with abandonment issues is to have unhealthy attachment styles that include: avoidant attachment, anxious attachment, and disorganized attachment.

AVOIDANT ATTACHMENT STYLE

People with an avoidant attachment style tend to avoid letting people get close to them. They essentially set up barriers to intimacy and self-isolate and are "distant, private, or withdrawn."[21] Furthermore, distrust is a huge factor in their engagement with others. They trust no one. Every interaction with familiar and unfamiliar people is a game of constantly analyzing, filtering, and dissecting the other person's actions toward you. Every word is examined, and a person's intentions evaluated. Is this person safe? How much do I let them in? Are they sincere? Yet in the end, you never really feel secure enough to fully give your heart to anyone, and that protective wall is always there.

Additionally, there are those who move from relationship to relationship and friendship to friendship to avoid attachment, disappointment, and hurt. As a common default the easiest way to avoid conflict and overcome one's fear of commitment is to simply withdraw or leave.[22]

ANXIOUS ATTACHMENT STYLE

"People with an anxious attachment style cope with fears of abandonment by latching on to others and developing intensely close and codependent relationships."[23] They often demonstrate clinginess, neediness and failure to place healthy boundaries between themselves and those they are connected to. They tend to stay in ongoing toxic relationships of all sorts longer than they reasonably should. This applies to romantic relationships but may very well apply to familial ties, friendships, and work relationships as well, especially with abusive or manipulative superiors.

It is interesting that those with anxious attachment styles may expend excessive energy in pleasing others but they themselves may be difficult to please. The individual may be overly critical of very minor things. Conversely, while they may be hypercritical of other people, they themselves cannot accept criticism. They are extremely sensitive to correction and downright defensive against any sort of critique. Driven by emotion, those who operate in the anxious attachment style misinterpret arguments, conflicts and disagreements of any type as a signal of being abandoned and as such resort to fear-based behavior to prevent it.[24]

DISORGANIZED ATTACHMENT STYLE

The disorganized attachment style is complex and spans both ends of the spectrum. People with a disorganized attachment often lack empathy and find intimacy and closeness uncomfortable.[25] As the title describes, there is disorganization and inconsistencies in the way a person behaves and responds in relationships in that they may exhibit either the anxious or avoidant attachment styles at various times and in varying degrees. Antisocial, narcissistic, or borderline personality traits and disorders are sometimes associated with the disorganized attachment style.[26]

To summarize, to live with abandonment is to constantly live in a posture of fearful defense. We are obsessed with being proactive in preventing repeat abandonment. The turning point for an abandoned person in a relationship, especially romantic, usually hinges on any perceived disrespect or sign of possible abandonment by the other party. For example, things may be going well in the beginning. But any change in the normal routine that triggers insecurity—such as a failure to call, failure in responding to a text, or even a partner taking some much-needed alone time—may activate unhealthy emotions and behaviors.

Bear in mind that some of the examples mentioned are the norm in everyday interactions and are often typical in any relationship. Indeed, there are times when a person cannot respond immediately, and of course, nothing is wrong with taking some healthy space. However, in such cases, the abandoned individual may display the demanding clinginess of the anxious attachment style or the distancing of themselves seen in the avoidant style. Additionally, they may take the route of self-blame as the reason for the other party's lack of affection, leading to exerted efforts to transform themselves into the person that they think will be pleasing to the other party. These types of responses may place a heavy strain on any relationship, pushing the other party away and ultimately resulting in the outcome of abandonment that the abandoned person was fighting so hard to prevent. Do you see what a vicious cycle this can become? Can you feel the fatigue of living the life of one who feels abandoned?

For those who have abandonment issues, you do not have to continue in this cycle. You do not have to continue to live out unhealthy relationships. God designed you to enjoy secure attachments with healthy interactions and fruitful relationships in all facets of your life. You can ditch abandonment today and begin to live in the freedom and fullness you are destined to live.[27]

Food For Thought:

1) *Name a few of your biggest fears.*

2) *What are some things that make you anxious?*

3) *Where do your fears and anxieties come from?*

4) *Can you connect any of them to abandonment issues? Pray and ask God to show you.*

CHAPTER 7:

IMPOSTER SYNDROME

Through honor and dishonor, through slander and praise.
We are treated as impostors, and yet are true.
(2 Corinthians 6:8 ESV)

For as long as I can remember, I have experienced some feeling of imposter syndrome. Yet, I didn't have a name for those feelings until I came across the term while talking to a family member in the spring of 2021. Though I don't recall all of the details in the conversation, she mentioned imposter syndrome as something she struggled with, and in the context of our discussion, I was able to develop a vague idea of what it meant. As I later researched more, I was astounded by how much it described me.

So you may be wondering, What is imposter syndrome? Although it is not an official psychiatric disorder that can be diagnosed based on the DSM-5, imposter syndrome is "characterized by persistent doubt concerning one's abilities or accomplishments accompanied by the fear of being exposed as [fraudulent] despite evidence of one's ongoing success."[28] It is the feeling that you are undeserving of the achievements you have made, the high esteem you are held in, or the respect you are given.[29] Essentially it is feeling unworthy of the blessings or good things that have come into your life, even if you have earned them partially through your own hard work. Central to imposter syndrome is the notion of the individual perceiving themselves as a counterfeit. It is the misconception that you are not talented enough, gifted enough, or as capable as people see you, coupled with this constant looming fear that once your shortcomings are discovered, you will be perceived as an imposter.

Factors that contribute to the development of imposter syndrome include a lack of positive affirmations especially in childhood and an environment of constant criticism in early development. Pressure to achieve academically and in competitive high stress environments at work, sports, and other settings are also contributing factors.[30] People with abandonment issues may struggle with imposter syndrome because common to both are feelings of low self-esteem, low self-value, and unworthiness.

PREVALENCE OF IMPOSTER SYNDROME

Imposter syndrome is more common than you may realize and is more prevalent in what are considered high-achieving professions. Imposterism may be found in approximately 25 to 30 percent of high achievers, such as doctors, lawyers, and CEOs.[31] Separate from high achievers, research suggests around 70 percent of adults may experience a period of imposter syndrome at least once in their lifetime.[32]

WHAT TRIGGERS IMPOSTER SYNDROME?

One main trigger of imposter syndrome is bringing attention to the person's achievements. Promotions, receiving awards, passing exams, or any other special recognition can initiate imposterism. Because the supposed imposter feels undeserving, highlighting or rewarding their abilities only works to fuel the feelings of unworthiness. A second trigger may be failure after an abundance of success. Of course, failure is an inevitable part of life.

> *It's called the impostor syndrome. It's almost like the better I do, the more my feeling of inadequacy actually increases, because I'm just going, Any moment, someone's going to find out I'm a total fraud, and that I don't deserve any of what I've achieved.*
> *(Emma Watson, Actress, Model and Activist)*

It is unrealistic for any person to expect to constantly excel, win, or succeed at anything on an ongoing basis. Yet according to an article written in *Psychology Today*, for the imposter, unexpected failure may cause them "to critique and question their overall aptitude."[33]

As an aside, it is important to recognize that those who deal with imposter syndrome often suffer from perfectionism and neuroticism. Perfectionism is, as the word implies, a constant striving for perfection driven by the fixation of accepting nothing short of being flawless. Perfectionists are often ambitious, hardworking, and focused, which can work in their favor. However, their dysfunctional fixation with achieving whatever their perceived standard of perfection is can be limiting in their progression and completion of what they aim to accomplish.

People who deal with imposter syndrome may also be neurotic. Neurotics are prone to negative emotions. Symptoms of neuroticism include being easily disturbed, excessive worry, frequent mood swings, feeling down, and increased irritability. Consequently, with neuroticism comes an increased risk of anxiety and depression.

Finally, people who deal with imposter syndrome have trouble accepting compliments or affirmations. They in essence downplay their gifts, talents, and skills. For the person who struggles with imposter syndrome, success or achievements are attributed to outside factors like a spiritual force, luck, or good fortune.[34]

Let me preface this by saying there is nothing wrong with acknowledging, for instance as it relates to my Christian faith, God as the source of my success because we truly cannot do anything without God's provision. However, it is incorrect to not acknowledge your contributions to your own success by failing to recognize such factors as: intentionality in utilizing your gifts, development of skills, consistency, determination, and endurance in mobilizing what God has given you. To do so is to show a level of false humility.

In my own experience, I am authentically a humble person by nature. Yet, I came to recognize that some of my aversion to praise or not receiving compliments well could also be attributed to a false humility associated with imposter syndrome. In my case, the idea of a false self also plays into imposter syndrome as well. The false self I presented to the world was one who was confident, courageous, and self-assured with everything intact when in fact deep down I was often fearful, anxious, and unsure of myself in many ways. Hence, it was hard to receive accolades, praise, or compliments because I knew who I really was.

Yet, as I came to experience more healing within, I allowed myself to accept the normalcy of being flawed. At the same time, I also began to celebrate my gifts, talents, and skills that are not only God given but that I have contributed to developing through my own hard work, time, and sacrifice. I am deserving of my accolades just as you are deserving of yours. For so many, imposter syndrome may be a primary symptom of abandonment issues. But don't let it continue to be your downfall. You can have victory over abandonment issues and imposter syndrome to embrace the greatness you have within!

CHAPTER 8:

SPECIAL CIRCUMSTANCES OF ABANDONMENT

Have I not commanded you? Be strong and courageous.
Do not be afraid; do not be discouraged, for the LORD your God
will be with you wherever you go.
(Joshua 1: 9 NIV)

I want to highlight two unique circumstances of perceived abandonment related to grief or disappointment that are important to be aware of. These scenarios may seem unrealistic or irrational, but to the one who feels abandoned, they can be a very real and personal trauma.

The two circumstances I am talking about are feeling abandoned by a deceased loved one and feeling abandoned by God.

FEELING ABANDONED BY THE DECEASED

Feeling abandonment by a deceased loved one is an experience I encountered when a very close friend lost a parent. For the sake of privacy and respect for this individual, I will present a hypothetical scenario that is based on real events. Sheila was an only child, and for many years, it was her and her father alone doing life together. They were each other's primary source of support in every way, and their lives were deeply intertwined. Sheila watched her father undergo a lengthy battle of bodily deterioration and repeated sickness over several years, and she became her father's faithful caregiver. Additionally, several times her father had near-death experiences, but by God's grace and his determination to live, Dad beat the odds and bounced back repeatedly.

The feeling of abandonment is like being left to fend for yourself in a world that doesn't care. (Lauren Oliver, Author)

So on that fateful day when Sheila's father passed away, it was a shock to many but especially to Sheila. Dad had always managed to pull through, and it was assumed he would overcome once again. But this go around, the Lord said it was time. Dad did not wake up but instead went on to be with the Lord. Besides the obvious grief that comes with such a devastating loss, more than anything, Sheila shared that she felt a deep sense of abandonment. In her mind, her father had always held on and kept living for her because he knew she needed him. He was her rock, her support, and her greatest

SPECIAL CIRCUMSTANCES OF ABANDONMENT

cheerleader. Yet even though she knew her father had endured many challenges in fighting illness over the years, his death felt like he had given up and abandoned her.

Feeling abandoned by a loved one who has died is not an uncommon phenomenon. Although it can be seen with any loss, anecdotally it appears to be more prevalent in cases of unexpected death or loss of close or immediate loved ones including friends and especially in child/parent relationships. The one who feels abandoned in their sadness may experience the typical stages of grief including denial, anger, bargaining (looking for a way to change the reality of the death or make it go away), and depression, but quite often anger, rage, or disappointment over the loss is specifically directed at the deceased individual for "leaving."

If you are experiencing a significant loss, I want you to know that in those moments of navigating pain and grief, it is ok to feel a sense of abandonment. Take the time to work through these feelings and the deep hurt associated with it. It often helps to do so with a trusted friend, family member, or mental health professional. However, if this type of outlook is prolonged or leads to dysfunctional behavior such as depression, anxiety, psychosis, or interference with normal daily function, then professional mental or psychiatric interventions may be warranted.

FEELING ABANDONED BY GOD

Perhaps you can relate to any of the following scenarios. You have been praying for something for a long while, even years, and your prayers have not been answered. It could be saving a wayward child, fixing a broken marriage, or believing for a financial breakthrough. Or perhaps you have been experiencing significant trials in your life—you lose your house, you are diagnosed with a serious illness, you have just been laid off, or there is the unexpected death of a loved one. It seems like one catastrophe after another with no reprieve. Or it could be the case that you experience discrimination at work, you have a boss who regularly mistreats you, or you may be overlooked for a promotion that you know you are deserving of.

With the challenges of everyday life and a world filled with such devastation as natural disasters, war, poverty, violence, disease, and death, it understandably leads one to wonder, "Where is God? Does He see? Does He care?"

It may seem like God has abandoned us. It may feel like He is silent, unconcerned, or oblivious to our plight. We are not seeing the results we hope for, circumstances don't change, and it appears evil is running unhindered through the land. Has God left us? Is He with us? Does He hear? But it is in these moments we must know that God will never abandon us. It is not His nature to abandon what He loves. The Bible says, "God is an ever-present help in times of trouble" (Ps. 46:1) and "He will never leave or forsake us" (Heb. 13:5). Sometimes God may for a time intentionally withdraw His presence from us. It doesn't mean that He has completely left us. But let's just say He becomes less obvious and visible in our everyday lives. He does so as a means of testing our faith, developing our trust, and increasing our dependence on Him. He wants to be

SPECIAL CIRCUMSTANCES OF ABANDONMENT

the first and primary love of your life. Remember God wants an intimate relationship with you.

Other times, God seems silent because He is working in the background to bring answers that will come in His perfect timing and a solution far better than we can imagine. For the Christian specifically, the Bible says, "And we know that all things work together for good to those who love God, to those who are the called according to His purpose" (Rom. 8:28 NKJV). It means for those who follow Christ, God can take the most challenging, evil, catastrophic circumstances and work them for your good—to bless your life, make you a better person and bless others around you. Often our greatest miracles come through our darkest hour, and our greatest purpose comes through our greatest pain. Allow God to take your deepest hurt and use it unpredictably for something good.

Lastly, it may seem God has abandoned us simply because God's ways are beyond our limited human understanding (Is. 55:8-9). It is the devil's primary aim to separate us from God, and he does so by telling us lies about who we are and who the Lord is. Promoting lies that cause us to question God's love, faith, and commitment are yet another one of Satan's deceptive tactics.

God is eternal, all-knowing, and all-powerful. His ways are far above our ways of thinking and being. We must accept the times when God moves or allows things to happen contrary to how we want while also recognizing that we will never have all of the answers we are seeking. The world is not yet fully restored

81

because Jesus has not yet come back. One day, He will return to make all things right. Until then, we will endure suffering, pain, and challenges in this life. Yet we can trust that God's faithfulness, love, and mercy are unfailing. And in doing so, we commit to following Him forward even in our hurt, disappointment, or lack of understanding because of the assurance of His goodness. God is still good!

CHAPTER 9:

STEPS TO VICTORY

"For I know the plans I have for you," declares the Lord, "plans to prosper you and not to harm you, plans to give you hope and a future." (Jeremiah 29:11 NIV)

You may recognize yourself within the pages of what I have written thus far. You may have had an *aha moment* or a revelation that indeed you could be struggling with abandonment issues. You may be asking where you go from here. Let me give you some key tools that are crucial steps in gaining victory over abandonment issues.

ACKNOWLEDGE THE TRUTH OF ABANDONMENT ISSUES

Let me start by saying if you recognize that you suffer from abandonment issues, then congratulations! You have taken the first vital leap on the journey to your healing. The initial step in fixing any problem is to first identify there is one. Now you may be tempted to ignore the subtle or not so subtle truth that abandonment is a struggle for you. You may try to dismiss what is in plain sight or what God is showing you about yourself in the words of this book. But if God is highlighting the heartache, He wants to bring you to your healing. There is no shame in having abandonment challenges. None of us are perfect. We all have faults we must face and flaws to overcome. So I encourage you today to embrace where you are in order to move forward in a steady path to healing and wholeness. The Lord wants to set you free. You don't have to remain in bondage to abandonment. Your breakthrough starts by acknowledging and accepting the truth.

ACCESS THE ROOT OF ABANDONMENT

Begin to look back to discover the root of your abandonment mindset and where it stems from. In reflecting and answering the questions throughout the book, you have already started the process. First, you may have to think back to childhood to investigate the culture of your family. Every family has norms or ways that are accepted in their family structure. For instance, some families promote being very secretive and discourage sharing secrets outside of the family unit. Other family cultures are very overprotective of their members. These types of families fret and worry incessantly over those seen as the children in the family, even after they have reached adulthood, thereby promoting an unhealthy fear of the unknown or fear of misfortune. These are just some examples of family culture and familial norms.

STEPS TO VICTORY

Additionally, try to identify key moments where you may have been or felt as if you have been abandoned. Was a parent physically or emotionally absent or neglectful or failed to be nurturing? Did your best friend move away or a beloved family member die, making you feel as if you were left behind? Has the love of your life left you to pursue another person? Or perhaps there were certain negative phrases that were said to you over and over that have become a normal part of your thinking pattern and enforce the negative image you see of yourself. Abuse of any kind—whether physical, sexual, emotional, or verbal—has devastating effects on many aspects of our mental and emotional health and can certainly lead to abandonment issues. Unearthing the root of the abandonment issue can be helpful in the healing process and in preventing repetition of those unhealthy behaviors in our children or future generations.

FORGIVENESS

You may find that you harbor some bitterness or resentment for those who may have hurt you through abandonment. The famous saying about unforgiveness being like *drinking poison and waiting for the other person to die* is quite true. Unforgiveness stores up bitterness in our hearts, leads to unhealthy thoughts and behaviors and ultimately takes a mental, spiritual, and sometimes physical toll on our bodies. Instead of punishing the offender, we end up punishing ourselves. Forgive because God has forgiven you and He commands us to forgive others.[35] Let God handle the person who has hurt you, and ask Him to assist you in truly releasing hatred for them out of your heart. In forgiveness, you will not only find freedom from abandonment but freedom from the overall detrimental effects of unforgiveness as well.

ALTER THAT ABANDONMENT MINDSET

Though others may have different religious views, I believe this book will help both Christians and non-Christians alike in overcoming abandonment struggles. No matter who you are or what you believe, you must begin the work of changing that abandonment mindset. It starts by looking at your Creator and what He says about you. I stand firm in my belief in God as Creator and that the only way to eternal life and full restoration of our relationship with Him is through the repentance of our sins and the acceptance of Jesus Christ as our Lord and Savior. However, the beauty is in His Word (the Bible), and whether you accept Christ or not, God says some special things about *all human beings.*

First, God says that humankind is made in His image (Gen. 1:27). Believe it or not, this really is an extraordinary fact. It does not mean we are God, which some people falsely believe, but as His image bearers we have some of the same qualities as God (to a lesser degree), which makes us the pinnacle of the created order. God has gifted us with creativity, imagination, the ability to love, intellect, wisdom, choice, and so much more—qualities that the Triune God carries Himself. So, the next time you feel unworthy or incapable, hold your head up and lean into the truth that you are wonderfully made in the image of God, a unique stamp that stands out among all creation.

Secondly, God says His creation, including you, is good. In fact, from the beginning God says His creation is indeed "very good" (Gen. 1:31). As discussed before, because of the fall, through the sin of Adam and Eve, every single person from the time we are born into this world possesses a sinful nature and is prone to wrongdoing. Yet despite this reality, at a minimum, as a part of His creation, the Lord sees you as valuable.

> *For I am sure that neither death nor life, nor angels nor rulers, nor things present nor things to come, nor powers, nor height nor depth, nor anything else in all creation, will be able to separate us from the love of God in Christ Jesus our Lord. (Romans 8:38-39 ESV)*

You are an object of His love. He made you with good intentions, and He has good plans for you. Despite your faults, your shortcomings, or your mistakes, God loves each one of us unconditionally because of His character and who He is. Good or bad, pure or evil, God loves you, and as such, His love and goodness are available to everyone.

However, Christians who exercise their free will by accepting the gift of salvation through Jesus Christ (being delivered from sin and its consequences), repenting of their sins, acknowledging Jesus as Lord and Savior, and surrendering their lives to Him enter a special contract with God. Christians are not only guaranteed the promise of eternal life in heaven with Him after death, but we are considered God's children and not just a part of God's creation. As God's children, we enjoy the same rights and privileges of God's actual Son, Jesus Christ. As Christians, our identity[36] is rooted in Christ; God sees us as Christ and so loves us with the deep, fulfilling, perfect love He has for Christ. Furthermore, the Bible says we are "coheirs with Christ," meaning we enjoy access to some amazing blessings (Rom. 8:17). Jesus stands as ruler over everything in the universe, but as His coheirs, we are given the authority to rule as well, to counteract evil, to walk in great spiritual power, to heal, to be set free from those things that hold us in bondage, and to live a life full of abundance of all good things. As God's children, you can overcome hurt, abuse, poverty, and everything that is contrary to the life of blessing God has for you. God's peace and protection are yours!

Most importantly, you are not abandoned. You have been adopted into the family of God (Eph. 1:5; Rom. 8:14-16). When a child is adopted, the adoptive parents agree to be fully responsible for the care and nurturing of that child as if that child is biologically their own. You are not alone. God promises to never leave or forsake us. In fact, Jesus tells His disciples, and it extends to us as Christ followers today, that He is with them "always until the very end of time" (Matt. 28:20). We can invite Him into our situations. He wants to meet our every need and attend to our concerns. He wants to be a central part of our lives. He is with you.

So whether you are a Christian or not, God is always there and available. In that respect, you are never alone. God in His mercy chooses who He wants to help, even those who may not acknowledge or accept Jesus. But the progression to a deeper relationship with the Lord is based on your choice. As a non-Christian who is part of the creation, His love and mercy are still available to you, but you are not guaranteed access to His protection and presence. As a Christian who enjoys the status of being a child of God, you are never alone and you are guaranteed His presence and protection.

That's not to imply that Christians don't experience bad things or hardships in life. We live in a world that is fallen, and so all of us will experience hurt, pain, sickness, and disappointment. All of the hurt and pain of life will not go away until Jesus returns, demolishing all evil once and for all and establishing a new earth. But the good news, or the gospel, of Jesus Christ is that for those who accept Him as Lord and Savior, your life does not end after you leave this world. Your future is not to just suffer on earth and die. There is a better life after this, and even if you suffer on earth, God's presence will never leave you. You will be in heaven in the glory of His presence forever. You are guaranteed his protection in that the devil does not have the final victory over you. You are protected from spending eternity in hell. After this life, despite its challenges, you are guaranteed to have eternal life with Jesus where you will be whole, healed, and experience no more pain. You are not an orphan. You are not rejected. You are adopted into the family of God, and you are under God's care forever.

Lastly, to change the abandonment mindset, there are benefits from using affirmations. True healing of emotional hurt and a toxic mindset involves targeting the mind and the heart. It requires replacing those negative thoughts with positive affirmations and the truth of who God says you are. For everyone, remember you are loved. You are deeply loved by God. You are special to God. God has good plans for you. God values you. God wants you to have victory in every area and to have eternal life with Him.

Yet for the Christian, you can add that you are a beloved child of the most High God. You are adopted into the family of heaven who loves and backs you from all angles. You sit in high heavenly places entitled to abundance in all areas through Christ Jesus. Through the work and power of the Holy Spirit, you are becoming more like Jesus and a better you.

AIM FOR SELF-CARE

Make sure to indulge in self-care. Remember at the root of abandonment is a lack of healthy self-love and low self-worth. Take time to be selfish in a healthy way. Now I'm not promoting toxic selfishness, self-centeredness, and self-indulgence. But pull back on expending energy to please and perform to gain acceptance, and instead, find the balance of placing a focus on loving yourself. Make self-care a lifestyle not an event.

Besides pampering yourself or indulging in special activities, true self-care involves healthy caring for one's self in every area of life. Good self-care, for example, involves setting boundaries with those who may be draining and learning to say no and not always being available to everyone. It may also mean spending time alone for your peace, making your health a priority, and taking time once a week to unplug from responsibilities to enjoy rest, relaxation, and drawing closer to God (the Sabbath). Additionally, self-care involves being intentional about what you watch, listen to, and engage with as well as limiting what may be toxic or heavy to your soul. That may include restricting your intake of the news, cutting back on social media, and avoiding people who gossip or purposely incite trouble. These are just some of the ways that self-care can become a regular part of your life routine. Make self-care a priority in how you live.

ACCESS MENTAL HEALTH RESOURCES

Lastly, you may benefit from consulting mental health professionals for counseling and support services. Counselors, therapists, psychologists, and psychiatrists are invaluable resources available to aid you in processing through the complexities and pain of abandonment on the road to better mental and emotional health. Talking to a trusted friend or spiritual leader can also be helpful.

ALL ABOUT GOD

I have listed several strategies thus far that are helpful in overcoming abandonment. But none are fully effective without the power, presence, and assistance of the God of Jesus Christ. Without God's intervention, you are mostly left with limited self-help tactics and partial healing from abandonment struggles. I encourage you to seek God for help as He is key in every step of the journey. He can reveal the truth of whether you have abandonment issues, the root of them, the reality of your dysfunctional behaviors, and the steps to your victory. He alone has the power to fully restore, and the Holy Spirit is a trusted resource to encourage, motivate, and comfort you as you undergo the challenging work of healing. Spiritual practices such as prayer, praise, worship, Christian meditation, and fasting are all invaluable methods that help us focus, draw closer to, and tune into the presence of God.[37] The God of the Cross is essential in overcoming abandonment syndrome.

Of note: There may be instances where a person is afflicted with a dark force, a demonic spirit of rejection or abandonment that amplifies the person's abandonment issues. These individuals may require additional healing through what is called a deliverance process, where the demonic spirit is removed by the help of a deliverance minister or a person empowered by God to remove the evil presence. Pray to God to show you if this is the case in your situation. For further assistance, seek spiritual help through a church that does deliverance if necessary.[38]

CHAPTER 10:

CONCLUSION

Abandonment issues rob us of the best God has to offer us. They rob us of our peace as we live in fear and trepidation of being accepted and are constantly exerting efforts to gain love and validation. Notice I used the word *exerting* because living the life of the abandoned is a strain that will eventually take a toll on you in some way. They hijack us of the joy of self-acceptance, basking in the beauty of our uniqueness, and thriving in the gifts we have to offer to the world around us. They bar us from loving others well and receiving love fully.

Lastly, abandonment issues often derail us from living our full purpose. Besides the primary purposes of being created to love God and love people, we were all created with a purpose to impact the world around us. God wants to collaborate with you to bring healing and restoration on the earth and to reveal His love and power to the world. Many people are walking around empty and unfulfilled because they are living a life lacking purpose. What are you put on this earth to do? What is your assignment? If you need clarity and direction in discovering or diving deeper to unearth your life purpose, visit *www.spillingthetealifecoaching.com* to receive a free teaching gift on recognizing obstacles to purpose. I further invite you to schedule a free strategy call to see if we can serve you through our *Pivot to Purpose* program.

Remember God loves you unreservedly. He wants the best for you. He wants none of us to perish but all to accept Jesus and have everlasting life. So in addition to you gaining understanding about the devastation of abandonment issues, reading this book may have also highlighted your need for Jesus Christ and you are now ready to accept God's gift of salvation. Or perhaps you followed Jesus in the past and strayed away. If you have made the decision to make Jesus your Lord and Savior for the very first time or you are coming back to Him, repeat this prayer as you mean it with all your heart:

PRAYER FOR SALVATION

"Dear Heavenly Father,
I believe that Jesus died for me.
I believe that Jesus paid for my sins on the cross.
I believe that Jesus rose from the dead.
I ask you to forgive me of my sins.
I ask you to wash me clean of all sin.

CONCLUSION

> I put my faith and trust in Jesus as my only hope
> for living eternally with you in heaven.
> I ask Jesus to be my Savior and my Lord.
> I want to live my life for Christ.
> I understand that my salvation is not based on my
> works but on the sacrifice of Jesus on the cross.
> Thank you for saving me!
> Amen!"[39]

If you've said this type of prayer for the first time or you are coming back to Jesus after taking some time away, congratulations and welcome to the family of God! The decision to accept Jesus is a personal one, and God knows your intentions. Once you've made this decision, you can check out the organizations on the Additional Resources page for further prayer and guidance or you can contact a reputable church that truly loves the Lord and preaches the truth of the Bible. The wonderful fact is that it is easy to access worship services and other church activities virtually around the world from the comfort of your home. Life with Jesus is not meant to be traveled alone but together as a family: the church who honors and loves Him.

I sincerely hope this book has given you some additional insight, direction, and guidance to face and overcome the plague of abandonment issues. And I hope even more that you have come to understand that God loves you and wants to make you whole, especially through the sacrifice and work of His Son, Jesus the Christ. You are so much more than the abandonment you may have suffered. There is more for you than the pain you have endured. May God give you the strength to push forward to your healing. You can ditch abandonment issues and soar in the freedom and fullness that is rightfully yours!

God's blessings, peace and freedom be unto you.

Yours in freedom and fullness!

— Dr. Tanesha Lawrence, MD

BIBLIOGRAPHY

"Abandon," Merriam-Webster.com, https://www.merriam-webster.com/dictionary/abandon. Accessed March 11, 2024.

Anxiety and Depression Association of America (ADAA). "Anxiety Disorder-Facts and Statistics." Accessed April 15, 2023. https://adaa.org/understanding-anxiety/facts-statistics.

Dacres, Taneki. *Pocket Full of Victories*. New York: The Vine Publishing, Inc., 2012.

Fritscher, Lisa. "Understanding Fear of Abandonment." Verywell Mind. Updated November 13, 2022. https://www.verywellmind.com/fear-of-abandonment-2671741

Hurst, Nancy. "Separation Anxiety Disorder DSM-5 309.21 (F93.0)." Theravive. Accessed January 10, 2023.

https://www.theravive.com/therapedia/separation-anxiety-disorder-dsm--5-309.21-(f93.0)

"Identity. "Yourdictionary..com, https://yourdictionary.com/identity. Accessed October 15, 2021.

"Imposter Syndrome." Merriam-Webster.com, https://www.merriam-webster.com/dictionary/impostor%20syndrome. Accessed May 23, 2024.

Kramer, Stephanie. "U.S. has world's highest rate of children living in single parent households." Pew Research Center. December 12, 2019. https://www.pewresearch.org/fact-tank/2019/12/12/u-s-children-more-likely-than-children-in-other-countries-to-live-with-just-one-parent/

Lockett, Eleesha. "Understanding Abandonment Issues." PsychCentral. June 29, 2023. https://psychcentral.com/health/abandonment-issues

McLendon, Beth. "Prayer for Salvation." Inspirational Prayers. Accessed August 7, 2022. https://www.inspirational-prayers.com/prayer-for-salvation.html.

National Institutes of Health/National Library of Medicine/National Center for Biotechnology Information. "Impact of the DSM-IV to DSM-5 Changes on the National Survey on Drug Use and Health [Internet]." Accessed January 10, 2023. https://www.ncbi.nlm.nih.gov/books/NBK519704/table/ch3.t25/

Perry, Jackie Hill. *Holier Than Thou*. Nashville: B&H Publishing, 2021.

Psychology Today. "Imposter Syndrome." Accessed December 10, 2022. https://www.psychologytoday.com/us/basics/imposter-syndrome

BIBLIOGRAPHY

Reimer, Rob. *Soul Care: 7 Transformational Principles For A Healthy Soul*. Franklin: Carpenter's Son, 2016.

Schoenfelder E.N., Sandler I.N., Wolchik S., MacKinnon D. "Quality of Social Relationships and the Development of Depression in Parentally-Bereaved Youth." *Journal of Youth and Adolescence* 40, no. 1 (2011):85-96. https://doi.org/10.1007/s10964-009-9503-z

Shafir, Hailey. "Abandonment Issues: Signs, Causes and How to Overcome." Choosing Therapy, September 14, 2022. https://www.choosingtherapy.com/abandonment-issues/.

Stanford Medicine Children's Health. "Separation Anxiety." Accessed January 11, 2023. https://www.stanfordchildrens.org/en/topic/default?id=separation-anxiety-90-P02283

Villines, Zawn. "What to Know About Abandonment Issues." *Medical News Today*. Updated November 30, 2023. https://www.medicalnewstoday.com/articles/abandonment-issues

Winnicott, D.W. "Ego distortion in terms of true and false self." In *The Maturational Process and the Facilitating Environment: Studies in the Theory of Emotional Development*, edited by M. Masud R. Khan. Madison: International Universities Press Inc., 1994.

NOTES

INTRODUCTION

1. Merriam-Webster, s.v. "abandon (v.)," accessed March 11, 2024, https://www.merriam-webster.com/dictionary/abandon.

2. "Understanding Abandonment Issues," Eleesha Lockett, PsychCentral, June 29, 2023, https://psychcentral.com/health/abandonment-issues

3. "What to Know About Abandonment Issues," Zawn Villines, Medical News Today, updated November 30, 2023, https://www.medicalnewstoday.com/articles/abandonment-issues

4. "What to Know About Abandonment Issues," Zawn Villines, Medical News Today, updated November 30, 2023, https://www.medicalnewstoday.com/articles/abandonment-issues

5. Soul Care not only helped me to gain freedom from abandonment issues but also from so many other areas of struggle that have hindered me in my life. I am so thankful to Dr. Reimer, his team, and his ministry, which have helped hundreds of thousands of people like me gain emotional and soul healing. I encourage you to read Dr. Reimer's book: Soul Care: 7 Transformational Principles for a Healthy Soul. Some of what I write about reflects on what I learned through Soul Care as it more specifically relates to abandonment issues. Also check the link to his ministry below

for other helpful resources including his transformational Soul Care conferences.

Rob Reimer, *Soul Care: 7 Transformational Principles For A Healthy Soul* (Franklin: Carpenter's Son, 2016). Renewal International Ministries: https://renewalinternational.org

CHAPTER 1: GOD'S INTENTIONS . . . THE GENESIS

6. Jackie Hill Perry, Holier Than Thou (Nashville: B&H Publishing, 2021), 166.

7. For a gripping, informative, and easy to read book on sin, salvation, and Christ's love, I recommend the following resource written by my dear friend: Taneki Dacres, Pocket Full of Victories (New York: The Vine Publishing, Inc., 2012).

8. Crucifixion was a widespread practice used in ancient times starting around 500 to 400 BC as a severe punishment ultimately leading to death. There are many resources available that expound on the details of crucifixion and more specifically the medical implications that lead to such a slow and tortuous ending of life.

Check the additional resources page at the end of the book for some informative resources on crucifixion.

9. Gen. 28:15, Deut. 31:8, Josh 1:5, Josh 1:9, 1 Chron. 28:20, and Isa. 41:17 contain examples of God reassuring the early Israelites that he would not leave or abandon them. That same assurance is available to us through Jesus Christ today.

NOTES

CHAPTER 3: ROOT CAUSES OF ABANDONMENT

10. "Separation Anxiety," Stanford Medicine Children's Health, accessed January 11, 2023, https://www.stanfordchildrens.org/en/topic/default?id=separation-anxiety-90-P02283

11. Dr. Nancy Hurst, "Separation Anxiety Disorder DSM-5 309.21 (F93.0)," Theravive, accessed January 10, 2023, https://www.theravive.com/therapedia/separation-anxiety-disorder-dsm--5-309.21-(f93.0)

12. "Impact of the DSM-IV to DSM-5 Changes on the National Survey on Drug Use and Health [Internet]," National Institutes of Health/ National Library of Medicine/ National Center for Biotechnology Information, accessed January 10, 2023, https://www.ncbi.nlm.nih.gov/books/NBK519704/table/ch3.t25/

13. Stephanie Kramer, "US has world's highest rate of children living in single parent households," Pew Research Center, December 12, 2019, https://www.pewresearch.org/fact-tank/2019/12/12/us-children-more-likely-than-children-in-other-countries-to-live-with-just-one-parent/

CHAPTER 4: ABANDONMENT AND IDENTITY

14. Yourdictionary.com, s.v. "Identity," accessed October 15, 2021, https://yourdictionary.com/identity

Please note this definition has been removed from yourdictionary.com

15. For more reading on core lies that affect identity, check out Soul Care. Rob Reimer, *Soul Care: 7 Transformational Principles*

For A Healthy Soul (Franklin: Carpenter's Son, 2016), Principle # 1—Identity.

16. D. W. Winnicott, "Ego distortion in terms of true and false self," in The Maturational Process and the Facilitating Environment: Studies in the Theory of Emotional Development, ed. M. Masud R. Khan (Madison: International Universities Press Inc., 1994), 146-147.

CHAPTER 5: SHAME

17. I was introduced to the concept of toxic shame in reading Dr. Reimer's book Soul Care and through participation in his Soul Care ministry. For more insight on toxic shame and its relation to identity, refer to: Rob Reimer, *Soul Care: 7 Transformational Principles For A Healthy Soul* (Franklin: Carpenter's Son, 2016), 20.

CHAPTER 6: FEAR AND ANXIETY

18. "Anxiety Disorder-Facts and Statistics," Anxiety & Depression Association of America (ADAA), accessed April 15, 2023, https://adaa.org/understanding-anxiety/facts-statistics.

19. E.N. Schoenfelder, I.N. Sandler, S. Wolchik, D. MacKinnon, "Quality of Social Relationships and the Development of Depression in Parentally-Bereaved Youth," Journal of Youth and Adolescence 40, no. 1 (2011): 85-96, https://doi.org/10.1007/s10964-009-9503-z.

20. Lisa Fritscher, "Understanding Fear of Abandonment," Verywell Mind, updated November 13, 2022, https://www.verywellmind.com/fear-of-abandonment-2671741.

NOTES

21. Hailey Shafir, "Abandonment Issues: Signs, Causes and How to Overcome," Choosing Therapy, September 14, 2022, https://www.choosingtherapy.com/abandonment-issues/.

22. Ibid.

23. Ibid.

24. Ibid.

25. Ibid.

26. Ibid.

27. Dr. Reimer has an excellent chapter on fear with good scriptural evidence for the impact of fear and practical anecdotes for overcoming fear in Soul Care: 7 Transformational Principles For A Healthy Soul (Franklin: Carpenter's Son, 2016), Principle #6—Fear.

CHAPTER 7: IMPOSTER SYNDROME

28. Merriam-Webster.com, s.v. "Imposter Syndrome," accessed May 23, 2024, https://www.merriam-webster.com/dictionary/impostor%20syndrome.

29. "Imposter Syndrome," Psychology Today, accessed December 10, 2022, https://www.psychologytoday.com/us/basics/imposter-syndrome.

30. Ibid.

31. Ibid.

32. Ibid.

33. Ibid.

34. Ibid.

CHAPTER 9: STEPS TO VICTORY

35. Scriptures on forgiveness include Col. 3:13; Matt. 6:14; Matt. 18:21, 22; and Luke 17:3, 4.

For an excellent discussion on forgiveness, consult the following resource: Rob Reimer, *Soul Care: 7 Transformational Principles For A Healthy Soul* (Franklin: Carpenter's Son, 2016), Principle #4—Forgiveness.

36. For a rich, in-depth discussion on the Christian's identity in Christ, read more in: Rob Reimer, *Soul Care: 7 Transformational Principles For A Healthy Soul* (Franklin: Carpenter's Son, 2016), Principle #1—Identity.

37. A rich and informative resource on Christian spiritual practices is: Richard J. Foster, *Celebration of Discipline: The Path to Spiritual Growth* (New York: Harper Collins, 1978).

38. To learn more about demonization/demonic influence: Rob Reimer, *Soul Care: 7 Transformational Principles For A Healthy Soul* (Franklin: Carpenter's Son, 2016), Principle #7—Deliverance.

CHAPTER 10: CONCLUSION

39. Beth McLendon, "Prayer for Salvation," Inspirational Prayers, accessed August 7, 2022, https://www.inspirational-prayers.com/prayer-for-salvation.html

Scriptures on salvation: Romans 3:23; 6:23; John 3:16; 14:6; 1 John 2:3-6.

ADDITIONAL
INFORMATIVE RESOURCES

CRUCIFIXION

Bergeron, Joseph W. *The Crucifixion of Jesus: A Medical Doctor Examines the Death and Resurrection of Christ.* Suwanee: St. Polycarp Publishing House, 2018.

Rutledge, Fleming. *The Crucifixion: Understanding the Death of Christ.* Grand Rapids: Wm. B. Eerdman's Publishing Company, 2015.

Zugibe, Frederick T. *The Crucifixion of Jesus, Completely Revised and Expanded: A Forensic Inquiry.* New York: M. Evans and Company, Inc., 2005.

SALVATION AND DISCIPLESHIP

Dacres, Taneki. *Pocket Full of Victories.* New York: The Vine Publishing, Inc., 2012.

Foster, Richard J. *Celebration of Discipline: The Path to Spiritual Growth.* New York: Harper Collins, 1978.

Perry, Jackie Hill. *Holier Than Thou.* Nashville: B&H Publishing, 2021.

Organizations:
- Discipleship.org https://discipleship.org
- Cru https://www.cru.org/
- Bible.org https://bible.org

- The Navigators Ministry https://www.navigators.org

SOUL AND EMOTIONAL HEALTH

Benner, David G. *The Gift of Being Yourself: The Sacred Call to Self-Discovery.* Downer's Grove: InterVarsity Press, 2015.

Brown, Brene. *The Gifts of Imperfection: Let Go of Who You Think You're Supposed to Be and Embrace Who You Are.* Center City: Hazelden Publishing, 2010.

Reimer, Rob. *Soul Care: 7 Transformational Principles For A Healthy Soul.* Franklin: Carpenter's Son, 2016.